Silent Voices

Silent Voices:
Meditations for Holy Week

*From the Palm Sunday Procession to the
Easter Upper Room*

GREGORY S. ATHNOS

RESOURCE *Publications* · Eugene, Oregon

SILENT VOICES: MEDITATIONS FOR HOLY WEEK
From the Palm Sunday Procession to the Easter Upper Room

Resource Publications
An Imprint of Wipf and Stock Publishers
199 W. 8th Ave., Suite 3
Eugene, OR 97401

www.wipfandstock.com

PAPERBACK ISBN: 978-1-6667-7326-2
HARDCOVER ISBN: 978-1-6667-7327-9
EBOOK ISBN: 978-1-6667-7328-6

05/16/23

Contents

Preface: Silent Voices   vii

The '*Voices*' in Scripture: Tradition and Legend   1

Day One | Palm Sunday and the Passover Meal

Scripture: The Triumphal Entry Into Jerusalem   5

Scripture: Jesus and the Money-changers   10

Scripture: At Passover Jesus Washes the Disciples Feet   13

Day Two | In the Garden of Gethsemane

Scripture: In the Garden   19

Scripture: Judas Betrays Jesus With a Kiss   22

Scripture: Peter Attacks the Servant of the High Priest   24

Day Three | In the Courtyard of Caiaphus the High Priest: The Servant Girl, Peter's Denial, Pilate's Response

Scripture: The Servant Girl Confronts Peter   31

Pilate in the Courtyard of the Governor   35

Scripture: The Custom at the Feast   38

Day Four | The Dream of Pilate's Wife and the Release of Barabbas

Scripture: The Dream of Pilate's Wife   43

Scripture: Pilate Releases Barabbas   46

Day Five | On the Way to Golgotha

Scripture: Simon of Cyrene, the Unlikely Cross Carrier   53

Scripture: Mary at the Foot of the Cross   57

Day Six | Crucifixion and Entombment: The Centurion, Joseph of Arimathea, and Mary Magdalene

Scripture: The Centurion at the Foot of the Cross   63

Scripture: Joseph of Arimathea Asks for the Body of Jesus   68

Scripture: Mary Magdalene at the Tomb of Jesus   73

Day Seven | Sunday: The Roman Guard, Mary Magdalene, and the Emmaus Road Appearance of Christ

Scripture: The Tomb is Made Secure   79

Scripture: The Earthquake   81

Scripture: Mary Magdalene Visits the Empty Tomb   85

Scripture: The Disciples on the Emmaus Road   87

Day Eight | The Risen Christ Appears in the Upper Room: Doubt and Faith

Scripture: The Upper Room, Evening of the Third Day   95

About the Author   103

Preface: Silent Voices[1]

Holy Week is filled with voices. Those who speak challenge us—some through eloquence, and some through cowardice. Still others, those *Silent Voices*, cause us to wonder what they might have said or done. Named or un-named, silent or not, they all played a role in the most sacred and profound eight days in all of history.

The four Gospel accounts paint the historical picture of God's redemptive plan in broad strokes that have resonated through the centuries. Almost everyone knows the story, Christian or not. We can recount the high points, like a smooth stone skipping across the surface of a vast lake.

We see the hill of Golgotha, the three crosses, the soldiers, the weeping Marys. It is history—our history—but the dust, the grit, the sounds, the tears remain attached to 'those others' gathered inside and outside the Jerusalem walls.

We read the familiar sacred accounts we almost know by heart. We know what happened, why it happened, and who was involved. We have a basic idea through Scripture of the political and psychological underpinnings of the story, but the emotional motives that prompted their actions are a bit more illusive. In other words, we know the story, but not their story. What lies beneath

1. *Silent Voices* began as a Reader's Theater eight-voice drama for a Good Friday service. Subsequent iterations for churches in several states developed new voices, accompanied by large screen projections of classical art depicting each scene. Responses from audiences and readers encouraged the current form as a series of Holy Week devotional meditations. While 'Silent Voices' reflects the entirety of Holy Week, individual voices could be integrated into worship services for Palm Sunday, the Maundy Thursday Last Supper, Good Friday, and Easter.

the surface? In many cases Scripture leaves unsaid what became of those *Silent Voices* in the aftermath of the crucifixion.

These meditations are not an attempt, nor are they intended to rewrite Scripture, history, or theology. Scripture, history, and the resulting theological interpretations are established and accepted by all wings of biblical Christianity. Rather, they comprise thoughts and emotions that might have lurked behind the decisions that each character made. While we know what the prominent figures said and did, in *Silent Voices* it is primarily those voiceless characters that speak. In these monologues and dialogues the readers are asked to put themselves into the hearts and minds of the silent ones and give them a voice suggested by the circumstances of their place in the story. How would we have responded?

Their challenges in the redemptive story remain challenges for each of us today. Can we see ourselves in the soldier, the thieves, the Marys, John, Pilate, Peter, Barabbas—even Judas? Can we feel what they felt—how they gloated—how they hurt—why they made the decisions they made? Will we put on their dusty sandals and wear their blood-stained robes? Are we willing to walk their walk—to stumble, pronounce judgments, sputter denials, hear the taunts, wallow in grief—to be conflicted as they were conflicted—to feel what it felt like to pick up his cross, or nail him to it? These meditations challenge us to utter their condemning or consoling words, feel their shame or grief, and wipe away the tears coursing down their cheeks and ours.

Rather than skimming along the surface of the familiar story, we are compelled to immerse ourselves in their deep waters and examine our hearts from the perspective of 'in real time' events, and not rely on our '20/20 hindsight'. Their flesh and blood stories require of us a flesh and blood commitment, an emotional 'baptism' of sorts. Navigating these waters you may find yourself in agreement or disagreement, and that is precisely the desired point: what would you do?

The story begins with the disciples' entry into Palm Sunday Jerusalem, their spirits filled with Kingdom hopes. The drama ends in the New Jerusalem of the resurrection, their hopes fulfilled. In between, a cosmic battle rages between *Death* and *Life, Doubt* and *Faith*. Not everyone will survive the conflict.

Perhaps the title should read *Silent Choices* rather than *Silent Voices*. Their struggle two thousand years ago becomes our struggle today. Facing the Savior everyone must make a choice. In first century Palestine not everyone made the right choice. Unfortunately, that is also true for many of us in our own 'Palestines' today. While reading each of the soliloquies keep asking yourself how you would have responded, knowing what they knew. Thrust yourself into the presence of the Lamb and ask the most significant questions of the ages:

"Who was this man?"
"How would I have responded to his willing sacrifice?"
"How will I respond today?"

The 'Voices' in Scripture: Tradition and Legend

All but one of the Disciples (Apostles) died alone as martyrs throughout the greater Middle East. They traveled alone as far east as India, as far south as Ethiopia, north to the borders of modern day Russia, and as far west as Italy or Spain, bringing the message of the risen Lord to the known world. When facing the choice of renouncing their faith or dying for it, none chose the former. If they had recanted their faith to save their lives no one would have known. The resurrection was no myth; they had witnessed it and were transformed by it. Would eleven men die for the sake of a lie? One might consider their martyrdoms to be the greatest evidence in support of the actual resurrection of Jesus. Their testimony was as sure as their faith. Whatever doubts they had expressed when Jesus was led away to His crucifixion vanished when He appeared before them in the Upper Room three days later.

The disciples appear in the opening and closing pages of 'Voices', bracketing the voices of the silent participants mentioned in the New Testament accounts.

The Apostles, according to tradition:

Simon Peter: Crucified upside-down under Emperor Nero in AD 64 or 67

Andrew: Crucified in Patras, Greece, on an X-shaped cross

Thomas: Pierced with swords and died in India, AD 72

Philip: Martyred in Anatolia (Turkey), c. AD 80

Matthew: Stabbed to death in Ethiopia

Bartholomew: Flayed alive, then crucified upside-down in Armenia

James (Alpheus): Stoned and clubbed to death in Syria, or crucified in lower Egypt

Simon: Refused pagan sacrifice and was killed in Persia

Matthias: Replacement for Judas, Stoned to death in Georgia

James (Zebedee): The first to be martyred, executed under Herod in 44 AD

Thaddeus (Jude): Martyred, axed in Syria, AD 65

John: Exiled to Patmos and died of natural causes c. AD 100

Judas: Betrayed Jesus and hanged himself

The Seventy Disciples

In Luke, chapter ten, the Gospel author mentions *Seventy Disciples* (referred to as the *Seventy Apostles* in Eastern Orthodox tradition). They were students of Jesus, who appointed them and sent them out in pairs to bring his message to the known world. The number includes many of his original disciples augmented by others whose names are mentioned in the writings of *Hyppolitus*, who was a student of *Iranaeus*, himself a student of *Polycarp*, who was taught by the last living Apostle *John*. Later writers' lists included several of the characters who speak in *Silent Voices*.

DAY ONE

Palm Sunday and the Passover Meal

Scripture: The Triumphal Entry Into Jerusalem

Say to the daughter of Zion, 'Behold, your king is coming to you,
humble, and mounted on a donkey, and on a colt, the foal of a
beast of burden.'
. . . the crowd spread their cloaks on the road, and others cut
branches from the trees and spread them on the road.
And the crowds that went before him and that followed him
were shouting, 'Hosanna to the Son of David!
Blessed is he who comes in the name of the Lord!
Hosanna in the highest!'
And when he entered Jerusalem,
the whole city was stirred up, saying, 'Who is this?'
And the crowds said, 'This is the prophet Jesus,
from Nazareth of Galilee.'
(Matthew 21:5–11)

Observing the Procession, Lazarus Speaks

Mentioned only in the Gospel of John, Lazarus was the brother of
Martha and Mary, friends of Jesus. Four days after his death and
burial Jesus raised him back to life. According to many theologians
that miracle prompted the High Priest Caiaphas and the Sanhedrin
toward their efforts to kill Jesus. John Calvin wrote, "not only
did Christ give a remarkable proof of his Divine power in raising
Lazarus, but he likewise places before our eyes a lively image of

*our future resurrection." One tradition states that Lazarus fled to
Cyprus to evade being murdered, where he was appointed Bishop.
Other traditions link him to France.*

*One remarkable tradition states he never smiled in the final thirty
years of his life, haunted by the unredeemed souls he had seen during his four days in hell. While no account places him at the Palm
Sunday procession, he appears in 'Silent Voices' as an observer for
the purpose of describing what he witnessed of death as a precursor
to the escape from its consequences the crucifixion and resurrection
of Jesus would offer.*

I watch the procession. I know where he's going. I've been
there: a saturating, penetrating, unforgiving darkness. Such an
absence of light you no longer remember it.

So cold you feel nothing; coldness is you, trapped in an in-
ferno of ice.

You become the plague, the price for abandoning Eden, for
destroying a Perfect Creation—a tragic penalty for your foolish
desire to be like God, to *be* God.

All the joys of life—the birth of children, the games, delights,
aspirations, accomplishments, the friendships, love—all gone in
an instant.

Tongues burn fiercely. Throats become inflamed. One is
struck dumb. Too late to confess guilt or beseech mercy. Too late.

Then decay. Flesh, fibers, tissue—all the connected strands
that make life suddenly unravel, untangle and spin away into the
frozen void.

Soon there will be nothing left but memory. Not the remem-
brance of what you once had in abundance; that is no more. There
will be no consoling memory of any joys that marked your journey. What remains is the inconsolable memory of what you refused to embrace: God's mercy, God's pardon. That tragic memory
will always be your prison; you will exist in utter darkness beyond
the only love that could have mattered. You will remember your
refusal, and be eternally haunted and condemned by it.

This abyss is Hades—Death—eternal separation. You loathe it. Fear it. Pretend it doesn't exist. Not for you, you say. But it waits . . . hungrily. It devours you. There is no escape.

I know; I was almost there.

My sisters, grieving at my passing, threw themselves at the feet of Jesus, crying,

> "If you had been here our brother would not have died."

Then, at that instant—as I neared my precipice of no return—I heard it: a soft sound breaking through my cold and dark separation—weeping! Their friend, weeping!

I thought his weeping was for me; but no, the tears seemed to have a greater purpose. He was lamenting his lost Creation and the monumental price he would willingly pay to rescue it. And I was the first recipient, the first to hear it.

Oh, the sound of his weeping can wake the dead.

I know it to be true! It woke me, bound in my Bethany shroud. Feeling began again; it was as if Adam's arrogant disobedience was being reversed in my disintegrating body! All my essence, all my being, all those broken strands—re-gathering! My descent into the unforgiving deep was being arrested, and I began to rise from that bottomless abyss! It was as if the tears he shed were becoming life itself.

I felt myself being mercifully drawn closer to what I had foolishly and recklessly abandoned, and then . . . a voice, a faint voice rose out of the weeping, more like a vibration I could feel than a word I could understand. Syllables formed slowly, gathering intensity, swirling throughout creation, stirring the still air of my tomb, cracking the ice that enslaved me.

> "La . . . za . . . rus."

My name! He called my name!

> "La . . . za . . . rus . . . . Lazarus . . . come forth."

There was light! I could see it! Warmth, I could feel it!

How is this possible? What power is this that overthrows the consequence of my foolish choices? Death's iron grip began losing its fight against the weeping voice that compelled me upward. I was soaring into a new universe; the cosmos began shouting a redeeming refrain, and all Creation joined in:

Death, where is thy sting? Grave, where is thy victory?

I was becoming the miraculous exception to nature's paradigm! I was becoming the first hint of what his journey would accomplish—the journey that begins today, as the crowds gather and sing together:

"Blessed is he who comes in the Name of the Lord!"

Now, as I stand aside, observing, he rides in humility through the throbbing streets of the Holy City. I watch his prologue to Creation's redemption. The crowds joyously anticipate his coming Kingdom unaware of what will take place five days hence. The Pharisees plot.

But I know where he's going—where he *must* go. I've been there.

I experienced Death's obscene power and its horror. I also received a greater power, a higher authority, one he will share—from his Father first—then with his Father. Death, thinking itself invincible, is about to be defeated. The promise of Genesis will be fulfilled: the head of his heel-bruising serpent will be crushed.

I know my life will come to another end, but no longer do I doubt the promise; it has already been fulfilled once in me. There will be another procession, a doorway to eternity. I will join another throng waving palm branches and singing 'hallelujahs' forever at the feet of my Savior.

So, you crowds desperate for a king, do not despair come Friday. At the end of his journey you too will feel the power of his weeping. You will hear the forgiving love in his tearful voice when he calls you by name. I know this because it happened to me.

"Come forth! Come forth!"

As I see him pass by, palm fronds obscuring his coming sacrifice, silent words form on my lips and shout from my resurrected heart,

Ride on!
Ride on in majesty, my friend, my Redeemer.
Ride on!

Questions:

Lazarus was granted a second opportunity to change the course of his eternity through Jesus, who demonstrated his resurrection power. We have one.
Have you heard His voice?
Do you believe the promise?
Have you embraced it?

Scripture: Jesus and the Money-changers

Jesus entered the temple area and drove out all who were buying and selling there. He overturned the tables of the money-changers and the benches of those selling doves. "It is written . . . my house will be called a house of prayer, but you are making it a 'den of robbers'."
(Mark 11:15–17)

The Pharisees Plot

Pharisees (Separated Ones) were the largest and most influential political-religious party in New Testament times. They controlled the Synagogues, religious education and worship. Pharisees were extremely fastidious in keeping the Mosaic laws, and by so doing changed the emphasis of Judaism from a religion of sacrifice to one of works. Outward appearance was of utmost importance (they're depicted as arrogant), and for that they were constantly criticized by Jesus. Keeping the 'letter of the Law' put them at odds with Jesus, who often performed miracles on the Sabbath.

A distinguishing characteristic, which set them apart from the Sadducees, was their belief in life after death and in bodily resurrection at the end of time. While considering themselves morally superior to the Sadducees they conspired with them to have Jesus crucified. Following the destruction of the Temple in 70 AD, the Sadducees drop out of the historical records, while the Pharisees establish the foundation of Rabbinic Judaism.

"Who does he think he is—God?"

"First he comes into our city thinking he's a King! His scruffy followers strut around the city like they own it."

"Tax collectors and prostitutes swarm around them like flies to donkey droppings."

"It's disgusting!"

"The riffraff of Jerusalem, that's what they are!"

"And then their idolized and self-proclaimed 'Messiah' . . . this . . . this fake god . . . goes into our Temple and upsets our traditions!"

"He says he has come to fulfill the law!"

"Worse, he says he is the law."

"What gives him the authority to challenge our time-honored ways? Who are his Rabbinic teachers? What right does this un-schooled peasant have to tell us what our Talmud says?"

"Has he ever prepared a sacrificial lamb for the purification of our people?"

"One of his followers, that wild baptizer, claims the Nazarene *is* the lamb that takes away the sins of the world."

"Preposterous!"

"He answers our questions with questions. Then he tells stories no one understands to change the subject."

"This . . . Nazarene points to us as objects of ridicule."

"Unwashed sepulchers?"

"Brood of Vipers?"

"We who have faithfully kept the laws and sacred traditions of Israel?"

"He must be stopped—but not by one of us. That will only enrage his adoring crowds."

"An insider . . . one of his . . . a weak link. Perhaps an incentive?"

"Money always works."

"We have it—silver. Thirty pieces."

Questions:

*Has 'religion' and its accompanying traditions
kept us from seeing the radical nature of faith itself?
Have our righteous 'works and deeds' obscured
our constant and necessary dependence on 'grace' and 'faith
alone'?*

Scripture: At Passover Jesus Washes the Disciples Feet

*Jesus said to them, "Go into the city, and a man will meet you
carrying a pitcher of water; follow him; and wherever he enters,
say to the owner of the house, 'The Teacher says, "Where is my
guest room in which I may eat the Passover with my disciples?"'*

. . .

And when it was evening he came with the twelve.
(Mark 14:13–14, 17)

*During supper, when the devil had already put it into the heart
of Judas to betray him, Jesus laid aside his outer garments, and
taking a towel, tied it around his waist. Then he poured water
into a basin and began to wash the disciples' feet.*

(John 13: 2–5)

The Upper Room Passover, Judas Speaks

*Judas, known as Iscariot, was one of the original twelve disciples
and keeper of the purse, notorious for betraying Jesus. He might
have belonged to the radical Jewish group, the Sicarii , hence his
name Iscariot. According to Luke 22, after taking the bread at the
Last Supper, Satan entered into him.*

*While he is known in orthodox Christian thought as Jesus'
betrayer, there have been various heretical attempts (including the
apocryphal 'Gospel of Judas') to portray him as a collaborator and*

close confidant of Jesus, the disciple strong enough to lead Jesus to His ordained sacrifice.

Though there are several versions of his death, one apocryphal story from the 'Gospel of Nicodemus' stands out: Judas, overcome with remorse, told his wife, who was roasting a chicken, that he was going to kill himself because Jesus was going to be resurrected, and when he was, would punish him. His wife scoffed and said God could no more raise Jesus from the dead than he could resurrect the chicken she was roasting. Immediately, the chicken was restored to life and began to crow. Judas ran and hanged himself.

'The kiss of Judas' has been a symbol of betrayal for two thousand years.

Everything was upside down. Rulers reign from above. Our leader was beneath us, sprawled on the floor. Kings don't shed their robes! Our 'king' was nearly naked, kneeling in front of us doing a servant's work. It was a humiliation. I was embarrassed to see him so degraded. I pitied him. I loathed him.

If I do not wash you, you are not in fellowship with me

. . .

And if I, your master, do this for you, then you must become as servants and wash one another's feet.

Women's work, not mine. Leave it to the Magdalene, that prostitute!

I was no longer in fellowship with him and I didn't care; my plan had just come together. The money was already in hand—thirty pieces. I pretended to go along with his absurd foot washing. Imagine it—a self-proclaimed king washing a peasant's dirty feet! Tradition and history were being turned on their heads; upside down, I tell you!

"You are now clean, but not every one of you."

He looked up at me when he said it. How did he know?

"Before the cock crows . . .

He knows it all ends tonight.

. . . one of you will betray me."

His words hung thick in the dense air over our Passover meal, punctuated by the confused "Is it I?" that screamed from eleven throats. This was no ordinary Passover meal, and they all knew it. Fear ruled the room:

"Is it I?"
"Is it I?"

First one, then the other, and on it went. I knew who it was, and could hardly contain my excitement about what was soon to follow.

I tore a piece from the loaf he held in his hands.

"This is my body . . .

Yes, and I now held that 'body' in my hands.

. . . broken for you."

I held the power of a new reality in my hands and dipped it into the cup he foolishly called 'his blood'. Soon it would no longer be symbolic; it was about to become literal. Passover? There would be no 'passing over' that charlatan tonight! Blood will be spilled. Not lamb's blood—his!

I held tight to the moneybag and silently left the confusion of the room. The frenzied *"Is it I"* trailed off into the distance as I crossed the Kidron valley into the darkness of the garden. I had a date with destiny—his and mine.

Questions:

How could Judas, who had seen Jesus' pure life and miracles first hand, bargain away faith for worldly possessions?
Has our faith ever been compromised by the attractive power of worldly things?

DAY TWO

In the Garden of Gethsemane

Scripture: In the Garden

And after singing a hymn . . . Jesus went with them to a place called Gethsemane. He said to his disciples, "Sit here, while I go over there and pray." And going a little farther he fell on his face and prayed, saying, "My Father, if it be possible, let this cup pass from me; nevertheless, not as I will, but as you will." . . . And he came to the disciples and found them sleeping . . . . (He) said to them, "See, the hour is at hand, and the Son of Man is betrayed into the hands of sinners . . . . My betrayer is at hand."
(Matthew 26:30, 36–46)

A Disciple Speaks

At the conclusion of our meal we sang the traditional Passover Psalms together. From our earliest Passovers we sang them in Messianic anticipation. We never suspected the prophecies would be fulfilled in our lifetime. But now? They were! We witnessed it just four days ago, as the crowd raised their voices, anticipating the song we were now singing:

> *"Blessed is the One who comes in the Name of the Lord."*

That was the Passover Psalm we loved. It was the other Psalm that had always confused us, the one about death and Sheol:

> *The snares of death encompassed me; the pangs of Sheol laid hold of me. I suffered distress and anguish. Then I called on the name of the LORD; "O LORD, I beg you, save my life!" (Psalm 116)*

We sang it, as we always did, but—snares of death? Sheol? As baffling as it was to us, we noticed a strange sadness come over our master's face as he sang. Did I see tears? What does he know? What does he see?

We left the upper room and crossed the valley into the quiet garden. He wanted to pray, by himself. Nothing unusual about that—he had done this as long as we had known him.

The night was peaceful.

His confusing words at the table seemed a distant memory now. The serenity of the garden settled our spirits even as the Psalm of blessing circled in our minds. It was quiet here on the Mount of Olives—thankfully. We soon forgot those haunting metaphors that had plagued us in the Upper Room:

> *"You will all fall away because of me this night . . .*
> *Body . . . Blood . . . Brokenness . . . Betrayal . . . Denial"*

The gentle wind whispered that Spring was in the air. The earth is being born again. New beginnings—not only for seasons, we thought, but for our Holy Land as well. Messianic deliverance! It was the promise that had possessed us for three long years.

We climbed to the midpoint of the garden. Someone was missing. Judas Iscariot. We hadn't noticed his departure from the upper room. He'll find us; he knows this is Jesus' favorite place to pray.

Finding a large rock, Jesus knelt by it, resting his bowed head against it. We rested nearby. The peacefulness of the garden and the night's tranquility suddenly were broken by his growing lament—something about his soul being grieved even to the point of death.

Then he came to us.

> *"Watch and pray."*

Pray, yes, we always did that. Watch? For what? We fell asleep—too much food, too much wine.

> *"Watch."*

We couldn't. His continuing cries from the rock fell on our deaf ears:

> *"My Father, will you let this cup pass from me? Thy will*
> *be done."*

We heard his plea in the distance, but it didn't penetrate our lethargy. Then, coming to us again, he said softly:

> *"The hour is at hand. Arise, the Son of Man is about to*
> *be betrayed."*

That last word roused us abruptly. Betrayed? *Betrayed*? It snapped us back to the stifling fear of the Upper Room:

> *"One who has dipped his hand in the dish with me will*
> *betray me."*

Shouts! Marching feet! We could see the lanterns and the mob in the distance.

The quiet garden became a scene of wild chaos: soldiers, spears, confusion—a kiss? Judas? Judas Iscariot! So that's who Jesus was referring to at Passover!

Questions:

The disciples slept in spite of Jesus' words of warning at the Last
Supper.
What warning signs surround us today? Are we aware of them?
Will we heed them?
How can we be prepared to withstand the world's ever increasing
assault on our Christian faith?

Scripture: Judas Betrays
Jesus With a Kiss

While he was still speaking, Judas came, one of the twelve,
and with him a great crowd with swords and clubs . . . . Now the
betrayer had given them a sign, saying, 'The One I will kiss is the
man; seize him.' And he came up to Jesus at once and said,
'Greetings, Rabbi!' And he kissed him.
(Matthew 26: 47—50)

Judas Speaks a Second Time

You think I betrayed him for the money. Not really!

It was those nagging doubts. Was he really who he said he
was? I know—I know you say,

"But what about the miracles?"

Yet doubts curled and slithered around inside my mind like
an insidious worm, devouring every fiber of my existence—the
reality of my three years with him obliterated by this unearthly
visitation. Satanic, that's what it was.

I remember one night as we were sleeping by the fire I awoke.
There he was, sleeping next to me. An awful vision began careening around in my brain: the memory of countless zealots in Israel
who had led people astray only to be captured and killed along
with their followers. I couldn't escape those images—those snarl-
ing voices; they kept pounding away at me:

*"He's a deceitful zealot! You should kill him now
and save us all from the anguish and wrath to come."*

I stopped myself.

*"But what if he is Messiah? Let it play out a little longer.
Give him more time to prove and establish his claim."*

Tonight at Passover Jesus' talk of dying was the final straw.
Satan was relentless.

"Messiah doesn't die."

There was a whispering in my ear; a rattling, gutteral, hissing
sound one hears at a deathbed:

*"Messiah sets up his kingdom. This imposter isn't Messiah.
Now, now is the time to strike."*

Don't ask me why I chose to identify him with a kiss. Betrayal
is one thing; I can live with that. If he isn't Messiah he deserves
to be stopped. But a kiss? A sign of affection—an affection I once
possessed in abundance? Turning that sign into something despicable? Using an intimate display of love to disguise and whitewash
an inner cauldron of hate—all for these silver coins burning my
hands and scorching my heart? I don't think I can live with that.

Questions:

*In how many ways have we denied the truth of Christ in our
daily lives?*
*Have 'kisses of affection' covered our animosities toward family
and friends, even those most dear to us?*

Scripture: Peter Attacks the Servant of the High Priest

Jesus asked them, "Whom do you seek?"
And they said, "Jesus the Nazarene."
Simon Peter therefore having a sword, drew it,
and struck the high priest's slave, and cut off his right ear;
and the slave's name was Malchus.
(John 18: 4—11)

The Servant Malchus Speaks

Malchus *appears in all four Gospels, but only the Gospel of John*
mentions his name, and only the Gospel of Luke mentions the
restoration of his ear by the miracle of Jesus. There appear to be
no traditions or legends that circulated about him; he is not heard
from again.

Yes, my name is Malchus, 'king'. What a joke! King? I am just a lowly servant, a slave of the High Priest Caiaphas, charged with honoring and protecting him and, if necessary, to lay down my life for him. I know my place. Me? Nothing. Him? Caiaphas? He is everything.

They had just finished their Passover meal. Their thoughts had not been on 'Messianic hope' but rather on revenge—revenge against this peasant blasphemer who claims to be the Son of God. Messiah? Nonsense!

Deliverance consumed their Passover conversations, but not the memory of deliverance from Egypt; they sought release from this imposter Jesus.

He surely is out of his mind! Delusional! Raging slanders filled the air:

> *"Messiah doesn't consort with prostitutes and tax collectors. He doesn't surround himself with uncultured fishermen—those crude ruffians with tattered goat-hair garments smelling of sweat, fish guts, and seaweed."*

What an un-royal, laughable entourage!

Just four days ago the sight of his adoring multitudes clogging the streets filled us with disgust. How could they be so deceived! Judas had seen the light, finally. We had seen it all along.

The time was ripe. We would strike tonight.

Judas knew his routine: a quiet garden under the blanket of darkness. The charlatan would be seeking a quiet place for his nightly meditations. Our disciplined and armed force would overwhelm his motley crew of ragtag fishermen. It was the perfect plot.

We left the palace and crossed the ravine where we met Judas. Our torches lit the way. We caught them by surprise.

> *"Rabbi!"*

Judas kissed their Master.

> **"Judas, is it with a kiss that you are betraying the Son of Man?"**

Him? He's the one? There was nothing intimidating or impressive about him—nothing regal, nothing suggesting power. The guards of our High Priest rushed to surround him. He stood in silence offering no resistance, but his eleven followers rose up in fury, screaming at Judas and attacking the attackers. Pandemonium ensued.

It flashed in the night air and I never saw it coming. I thought they were men of peace! Hadn't Judas assured us it would be an easy capture?

It flashed, the knife flashed, and in the turmoil my ear was severed. I simultaneously grabbed the bleeding side of my head and shouted pained curses at my attacker:

"You filthy spawn of a viper!"

I knew who it was. His reputation preceded him: irrational Peter, always the rabble-rouser living on the knife-edge of anger, they said, always acting before thinking.

For it is written, 'I will strike the shepherd and the sheep will be scattered.'
(Zechariah 13:7; Matthew 26: 31)

His friends thought he was brave, but after striking me he fled, slashing the darkness with his bloody knife. The others abandoned their 'so-called Messiah', running in several directions. Through my pain I screamed at them,

"Cowards!"

It became quiet. Then—I swear—something unexpected happened. Our captive bent down, picked up what the knife had taken, and placed it back on my bleeding wound.

He said nothing.

It was as if he was meekly assuming the role of a servant, a slave honoring and protecting his 'king'. Me? His king? Making himself nothing? Me, everything? The irony cut me like another knife.

The power of his gentle act shook my entire body—I could feel it. More than physical brokenness was being healed. There was an unspeakable force, an energy that bent my reality.

My ear was restored; my pain vanished! I'm telling you— believe me—it's true. At that moment my blurry world became intensely focused. Clearly, his act was not of human origin: his compassion even as he anticipated our coming vengeance was—I struggle to say it—Godlike. They said he was just a carpenter's son, but the power of his healing touch was miraculous and unearthly. Was he really God's son, just as he said? He must be. He had to be. I was becoming certain.

They must be wrong, I thought, all of them—Caiaphas, the Elders, Judas—all. I felt immediate guilt for consorting with them in this despicable plot. My screams began again; it was the pain of remorse strangling my heart. How can I live with what I am doing, delivering this innocent man to his ghastly slaughter?

I followed him at a distance as he was led away, repeating over and over again,

> "I must follow him no matter where it leads, even to
> death—
> either his or mine. Lord, I believe you are Lord.
> Remember me, my true King. I am your servant
> Malchus."

Question:
On the basis of Jesus' miraculous healing some have felt Malchus was convinced of the Kingship of Jesus, as suggested here. Are there 'miracles' in our own lives that have pointed us to the truth of Christ?

DAY THREE

In the Courtyard of Caiaphus the High Priest

The Servant Girl, Peter's Denial, Pilate's Response

Scripture: The Servant Girl Confronts Peter

Those who had arrested Jesus took him to Caiaphas, the High Priest . . . . But Peter followed at a distance . . . . And a servant girl came up to him and said, "You also were with Jesus the Galilean." But he denied it before them all, saying, "I do not know what you mean." . . . Another servant girl saw him, and she said to the bystanders, "This man was with Jesus of Nazareth." And again he denied it with an oath, "I do not know the man." After a little while the bystanders came up and said to Peter, "Certainly you too are one of them, for your accent betrays you." Then he began to invoke a curse on himself and to swear, "I do not know the man." And immediately the rooster crowed . . . and he went out and wept bitterly.
(Matthew 26:57–75)

The Servant Girl Speaks

The story of the Servant Girl and her confrontation with Peter in the courtyard is told in all four Gospels: Matthew 26; Mark 14; Luke 22; and John 18. She is never mentioned by name. Apart from the Gospels she is not mentioned in historical accounts. No legends or myths were created surrounding her character.

I saw him lurking in the shadows. His shifty glances darted from one face to another as he pulled his cloak over his head. Was that a knife jutting out of his waistband? Did I see blood? Better check. We've seen our share of attempted assassinations in recent years. Zealots have their followers, you know, and many are willing to die for their cause.

He moved further from the light of the fire. Hmmm . . . very suspicious. I cautiously moved closer. As I approached he retreated even further into the shadows. While pointing to the Nazarene, I confronted the intruder and shouted,

"I've seen you with him; you're one of his followers."
"I don't know what you mean."

There was an element of fear in his tone. As he tried to ward off my accusation he began slowly retreating toward the entrance to the courtyard. Another servant girl approached. Her accusatory comment was met with another loud denial, his voice fearful, high pitched and cracking—

"I never knew the man."

As he kept backing toward the exit a group of men surrounded him. Their intersection was more confrontational:

"You speak like a Galilean. Obviously you're not one of us. You're one of his."

Now, shouting against the mob, he peppered his denials with cursing and swearing. And with that, he roughly threw his accusers aside and bolted out of the courtyard. His cursing continued, growing ever more faint as he disappeared into the distance.

Accusations against the Nazarene echoed relentlessly within the courtyard. But what was that other sound—the sound that grew louder even as his denials vanished into the smoke-filled air? Screeching? Shrieking? It was the last thing I expected to hear in the middle of the night; it . . . sounded . . . like . . . *crowing*!

Peter, the Denier, Speaks

There is no more flawed and vacillating character in the New Testament than Simon Peter. His life is a rollercoaster between boldness and cowardice. He was the first to declare Jesus as the Messiah.

Then, after Jesus began speaking of his coming crucifixion it was Peter who said, 'No Lord, that can't happen to you.' It was Peter who defended Jesus on the night of his arrest by cutting off the servant's ear, and then a few hours later denied with cursing and swearing that he had ever known Jesus.

After his resurrection Jesus singled out Peter for attention, telling him he would die the same death of crucifixion, to which Peter didn't flinch. It was bold Peter who preached the first resurrection sermons in front of the enemies of Jesus, and thousands believed. It was a comforting Peter who wrote letters to the emerging Christian community encouraging them to be steadfast in the face of persecution and death. He insisted upon being crucified upside down, as he didn't think he was worthy of imitating Christ.

His remarkable transformation (no one is more deserving of condemnation than one who denies Christ) is an example of the pursuit, grace and forgiveness available through Christ. Peter is honored as the first Bishop of Rome and the first Pope of the Roman Catholic Church.

My name is Simon Peter—*Rock*. They all counted on me to be steadfast, bold. Yes, I was bold—and brash—but wasn't that a good thing? Remember when we disciples were fishing and saw Jesus on the shore? Didn't I leap out of the boat and walk on water? I actually did, until I realized what I was doing and began to doubt—then I sank. At Passover I promised I would fight for him, and I did, attacking the servant of the guard—I promised I would die for him, and I thought I could. Now? I wonder; I'm not so sure.

Here I was in the courtyard of the High Priest. You might say it was brash or bold to follow the soldiers to see what was happening.

Perhaps, but I found myself hiding in the shadows, away from the revealing light of the fire, using the smoke as another shield against discovery.

I was afraid. I wanted to be faceless, nameless. I formed my cloak into a hood. So much for 'rock'; so much for boldness.

I was discovered! I regretted my choice to follow him.

"No, I'm not one of them. No, you're mistaken."

Finally, swearing at the top of my voice, I shrieked,

"I never knew him!"

I bolted through the mob blocking my path and fled into the night.

Had he heard my denials? Had I caught a glimpse of him looking at me from across the courtyard—me, his strong one, his 'rock'? Was it a look of disgust? Sadness? Pity?

The heart-curdling sound of crowing echoed off the courtyard walls, a sound he had predicted, a sound that will haunt me as long as I walk the earth.

Grief swept over me as I stumbled through the dark streets. I wept bitter tears, flooded with salt and self-loathing. Just as I had doubted and sank in the Sea of Galilee, so now I was sinking once more into a far deeper sea of overwhelming despair.

Don't call me Peter again—or 'rock'. Tortured words formed slowly in the silence of my guilt, then spewed forth in a torrent of shame:

"My—name—is—'coward'."

Questions:

***Can we see ourselves in this account of the servant girl and
Peter?***
How often have we been the accuser? The accused?
In what ways have our actions and responses betrayed our faith?

Pilate in the Courtyard of the Governor

Pontius Pilate was the Roman Prefect (Governor) of Judaea who had a history of offending the Jews by bringing Caesar's image into the holy city of Jerusalem. He presided at the trial of Jesus and gave the order for his crucifixion. Pilate was ordered back to Rome to stand trial for cruelty under the charge that he had executed men without a proper trial. According to the early historian Eusebius of Caesarea, Pilate killed himself on orders from the Emperor Caligula. There are other accounts regarding his death from natural causes.

In the early Middle Ages church traditions created various stories about Pilate, including that he was a villain, or that he became a Christian to whom the risen Christ appeared, or perhaps that he was doing God's will by crucifying Jesus. The Gospels portray Pilate as reluctant to execute Jesus. He attached a notice to the cross which read, 'Jesus of Nazareth, king of the Jews'. Was it meant to mock the Jewish religious leaders, or was it a defense of Jesus and an admission of his kingship? When the leaders asked him to remove it, Pilate replied, 'What I have written, I have written.'

The Ethiopian Church and the Egyptian Coptic Church venerate him as a martyr and saint.

When they insisted on getting me out of bed so early this morning I thought it must be an urgent crisis. I expected to be confronted by someone who was a serious threat to Jewish leadership and the authority of Rome. I thought they must have needed the Roman legions to put down an insurrection by yet another deluded warrior claiming his right to be king. So I hurried from my bed, dressed, and rushed into the courtroom. Have to keep these religious leaders happy—have to keep the peace.

Imagine my surprise when they brought this poor, wretched carpenter's son to me. Now, I'm not a Jew; he is. He's one of theirs. In Rome we embrace our gods even if they don't mean much to us. It's the civilized thing to do. Here, they kill them. What barbarians!

"Caesar, get me out of this forsaken backwater, this—cultural desert.
Anywhere—just away from this small-minded race."

Look at him! He wears the homespun cloth of a peasant. His followers call him their king. King? Where is his shield, his crown, his signet ring of authority? He doesn't look like a king to me. Listen to his words; they have no forcefulness or power. Where is his chariot? Where is his army? He couldn't possibly overthrow even this impotent collection of priests and rabbis, much less the great empire of Rome.

If he were a real king I'd act swiftly, but there is nothing kingly about him. I find him no threat to me or to Rome.

Now Jesus stood before the governor, who asked him . . .
(John 18)
Pilate Speaks to Jesus and the Multitudes

"Are you the king of the Jews?"

"My kingdom is not of this world."
"So you are a king?"

"You say correctly that I am a king.
For this I have been born, and for this I have come into the
world,
to bear witness to the truth."

"What . . . is . . . truth?"

When he had said this he went out again to the Jews and said to them . . .

"I find no guilt in Him."

Scripture: The Custom at the Feast

Now it was the governor's custom at the Feast to release a prisoner chosen by the crowd. At that time they had a notorious prisoner, called Barabbas. So when the crowd had gathered Pilate asked them:
(Matthew 27:15–16)

Pilate Addresses the Multitudes

"Which of the two do you want me to release for you?"
    "Barabbas."
"Then what shall I do with Jesus who is called Christ?"
    "Let him be crucified!"
"Why, what evil has he done?"
    "Let him be crucified!"

When Pilate saw he was getting nowhere,
but that instead an uproar was starting,
he took water and washed his hands in front of the
crowd.

"I am innocent of this man's blood. It is your responsibility."
    "His blood be on us and on our children!"
They can do whatever they want with him. They say *Crucify*? Fine! Instead of a seat in the palace, let him wear his throne—a wooden throne. We'll nail him to his throne and write at the top he was king of the Jews. That insult should teach those chief priests

and rabbis not to disturb me in the middle of the night. Just let me get back to bed.

"He's yours to do with as you please. Go ahead, crucify him, but remember what I said:

I find no fault in him, so don't lay your guilt on me."

Questions:

What could Pilate have done to boldly defend Jesus if he truly believed he was innocent?
Is 'washing one's hands' of a situation enough to justify our actions?
Have we ever been guilty of doing that?

DAY FOUR

The Dream of Pilate's Wife and the
Release of Barabbas

Scripture: The Dream of Pilate's Wife

While Pilate was sitting on the judges' seat, his wife sent him this message: "Don't have anything to do with that innocent man, for I have suffered a great deal today in a dream because of him."
(Matthew 27:19)

The Wife of Pontius Pilate Speaks of Her Dream

Pilate's Wife, un-named in the Scriptural accounts, is mentioned in a single sentence in Matthew 27: 19. In the 2nd century the early Church Father Origen stated that she became a Christian. Two strange, non-Biblical theories surround her. First, that God sent the dream so that she would become a Believer. The second theory suggests the dream came from Satan in order to thwart the redemption that would result from Jesus' sacrifice; if Satan could keep Jesus from dying, God's plan for redemption would be stopped.

In the 4th century two Apocryphal writings, the 'Acts of Pilate' and the 'Gospel of Nicodemus', gave her the name Procula. 1300 years later she was given the name Claudia in the 'Chronical of Pseudo-Dexter'. Pilate's Wife is revered as a saint in two traditions: the Eastern Orthodox Church and the Ethiopian Orthodox Church.

He keeps pacing around the dark room, weeping. Mingled with the sobs I hear his words,

"Innocent—Guilty—Water."

Over and over again. Listen . . .

"Innocent—Guilty—Water."

My heart aches for my husband. I thought to myself,

"He really is a good man."

I try to convince myself. He was assigned to Jerusalem, this awful Jewish backwater, so far removed from the pleasures and culture of Rome. It was thought he could be a peace-keeper, a bridge builder.

All night my sleep had been tormented by the horrifying thought that all would come to ruin if this innocent Nazarene suffered. The voices in my dreams were relentless; I was being strangled by them. I pleaded with them,

"Let me be!"

I awoke, trembling, wet from exhaustion. I *must* tell my husband. What will I tell him?

I knelt by his side, begging him:

"Don't do anything to that man Jesus."

He said he had to keep the peace, even though he despised the political manipulations of the Sanhedrin.

"Surely the choice between Jesus and Barabbas will be an easy one for them."

He knew who was guilty and who was not, but he wasn't prepared for the hatred and animosity they held for the Nazarene. They condemned an innocent man to crucifixion.

"Innocent—Guilty—Water."

The litany of sobs and moans rack his soul. I ask softly,

"Who is innocent?"

I already knew the answer. He wails,

"Jesus, Jesus, Jesus."

Who, then, is guilty, I think to myself? Certainly not Jesus— and please, not my husband! I ask him—he says he is forever guilty for not standing up to the enemies of Jesus. I cannot dissuade him of it—nor myself.

He keeps rubbing his hands together as if he is washing them, hoping for a different outcome. He despairs, convinced there could never be hope for sentencing a righteous man to such a cruel and undeserved death.

My poor, good husband. I pray to my Roman gods, I beseech them,

> *"Spare this man, the man of my heart. Jupiter, Mithras,*
> *why are you silent?*
> *Answer me! (silence) I beg of you, answer me!"*

I dread the condemnations that will fall upon my Pilate, my bridge builder. I fear their future litanies, their creeds, these followers of Jesus, and I grieve:

> *"Crucifixus sub Pontio Pilato!"*
> *"Crucified under Pontius Pilate!"*
> *"Crucified . . . under . . . Pontius . . . Pilate!"*

Questions:

Pilate's wife was bold in confronting her husband and his authority.
Have we found ourselves in similar situations?
Have we been bold enough to stand for truth in spite of the consequences for doing so, or have we conveniently kept silent?

Scripture: Pilate
Releases Barabbas

Pilate, wanting to release Jesus, addressed them again;
but they kept shouting, "Crucify, crucify him!"
A third time he said to them, "Why, what evil has he done?
I have found in him no ground for the sentence of death;
I will therefore have him flogged and then release him,"
but they kept urgently demanding with loud shouts
that he should be crucified; and their voices prevailed.
So Pilate gave his verdict that their demand should be granted.
He released the man they asked for,
the one who had been put in prison for insurrection and murder,
and he handed Jesus over as they wished.
(Luke 23:20–25)

Barabbas, the Released Prisoner, Speaks From the Grave

All four Gospels refer to a Jewish custom that allowed the commuta-
tion of a death sentence by popular acclaim. Apart from the Gospels
no accounts of such a custom exist. Barabbas is mentioned in all four
Gospels. Unfortunately, his story has been used by some throughout
history to blame the crucifixion on the Jewish people as a nation,
rather than on a few of their self-serving leaders. Apart from his
mention in the Gospels no traditions or legends arose in history.

History treats me as if I never existed. Some say the Gospel writers invented me.

They couldn't be more wrong! I am not a figment of someone's imagination. I am real flesh and blood sitting in this cell waiting to be crucified. You call me an insurrectionist, a murderer. I prefer 'revolutionary'. I hate Roman occupation, and I'm not alone. We're freedom fighters. We despise the weakness we see in our fearful, timid leaders who roll over in subservience to those foreigners. Not us! We're willing to die for the sake of the nation.

The Romans keep killing us, filling crosses on all the roads leading into Jerusalem. But intimidation can't stamp out our attempts to rid our country of these oppressors. If it wasn't me in this cell it would be someone else, another revolutionary; a Barabbas substitute.

Some say we're after the same result, that peasant from Galilee and us. But don't mistake us for that Nazarene. Our acts are brutal. Hope? We kill for it. The Nazarene? He gives it away. No cost. No penalty. Absurd! The Romans ridicule such meek subservience, but they fear our harsh barbarism because they understand its persuasive power. They crucify. We assassinate. It's equalized brutality; that's why our actions stand a greater chance of success than his; that's why they *must* kill us. That's why I'm in this dank hole awaiting execution.

I was on trial. I could hear those voices in the courtyard. I heard my name over the tumult, and the cries . . .

'Crucify, crucify'.

Then footsteps—getting louder, approaching my cell! My body began to shake as the jailer set his key in the lock. I could taste fear heavy in my throat.

I know what crucifixion is; I have seen many. We revolutionaries are resigned to it. There is no greater torment one can suffer. It is a great price we're willing to pay for an even greater prize. Call us martyrs; it is our high calling.

But the glory of martyrdom doesn't make the thought of excruciating pain any easier to bear. Yes, my warrior's reflex will be to fight death on that cross with every fiber of my being. But I also fear I'll pray a weakling's prayer to whatever gods will listen to grant me a swift demise.

With false bravado I shouted,

"May my blood redeem our nation."

The lock sprang free. The sound of it was deafening. I could feel my courage shriveling.

The iron cell gate opened; the squeal of rusty metal on metal set my already jangled nerves into a deeper shock.

I hated the cowardice springing up inside me. I found myself collapsing in utter terror. My stomach was churning, gagging my throat. My weakness was humiliating. Cowering, I forced myself to look up at my executioners.

"No soldiers? No chains?"
"Pilate says you're free to go. They want to kill the self-proclaimed Messiah Jesus instead."
"But what about those voices I heard from the courtyard?"
"It was Pilate arguing with the Sanhedrin, declaring the Nazarene innocent."

So . . . Pilate was giving them a choice, thinking not even fellow Jews would defend a villain as despicable as me! Their vehement shouts of 'crucify, crucify' were not crying out for *my* blood, but *his*. Why do they hate him so much more than me? How could his rebellion be any greater than mine?

My crucifixion, the penalty I deserve is being transferred to the innocent carpenter's son, while his life of innocence is transferred to me? He dies a murderer's death while I, the murderer, go free? My infamy becomes his crown of thorns? He suffers the spikes in his hands and feet for my rebellion?

Who *is* this man? Why does he willingly take my place?

One would think my heart would change, that I'd become indebted to him, maybe even become a follower of his message. One would think I might renounce my acts of violence and submit to his gospel of peace. One would think I might claim him as my

Savior; after all, he will stand in my place when he wears that cross for my transgressions. One would think . . .

Well . . . history will record nothing of my life following my release. No legends will arise. No myths will be created. No one will seek to make me a saint. I'm just a guilty man set free to a life of obscurity by an innocent man whose sacrifice will change the entire world.

I disappear into the fog of the centuries. You know my name even if you don't believe I actually existed.

'Barabbas'

Can you even say my name without venomous contempt? You may see me; you may not. Only the end of history will solve this riddle.

But put yourself in my place. If you're another rebelling 'Barabbas' . . . if your sins against humanity and even against God were acquitted, and you were set free through an act of substitution and love . . . if this Jesus willingly took into his body the nails you deserved and the crucifixion you desperately feared . . . how would *you* respond?

Pity me—*pity me*—I made the wrong choice.

Questions:

*Barabbas had every opportunity to embrace Christ's substitutionary forgiveness, yet in his arrogance chose not to.
Have we ever relied on our own sense of 'worthiness' or 'righteousness' out of pride and ego?*

DAY FIVE

On the Way to Golgotha

Scripture: Simon of Cyrene, the Unlikely Cross Carrier

After having Jesus scourged they led him away to be crucified. On the way to Golgotha they seized upon a man called Simon from Cyrene, on his way in from the country, put the cross on his back, and made him walk behind Jesus.

(Luke 23)

Simon of Cyrene Speaks

Simon of Cyrene *is mentioned in the three Synoptic Gospels: Matthew, Mark, and Luke. Born in what is modern day Libya, it is thought he journeyed to Jerusalem to celebrate Passover and visit the Synagogue maintained by Cyrenian Jews. He became caught up in the Good Friday journey to the cross. It is unclear whether he was chosen to carry Jesus' cross because of his expressed sympathies for the Nazarene, or if he was simply in the wrong place at the wrong time.*

It is thought that Simon of Cyrene's two sons, Rufus and Alexander, became missionaries to Rome, suggesting that Simon had become a follower of Christ. His name appears on one of the lists of Seventy Disciples, along with the names of his sons.

Confusion everywhere . . . shouting . . . curses blackening the air. There was mob chaos, and it was spoiling my pilgrimage to Jerusalem. I had waited years . . . slaved . . . sacrificed for this once in a lifetime spiritual journey. It was to be the most sacred moment in my life with the God of Abraham, Isaac, and Jacob. Where was the solemn reverence I expected? Why these unruly gangs crowding the streets, blocking my way to the Temple? Who are they screaming at?

I forced my way forward, one hand parting the uncontrollable sea of insane humanity, the other holding tightly to my money belt.

Then I saw him.

His flesh hung in broken, bloody strands, still oozing. I could trace his gruesome journey by the bloody trail staining the stones. Who did this to him? Who placed that heavy wooden beam across his torn shoulders? Why? Why that ring of thorns forced upon his bleeding head? The image of his suffering was so intense it made my own flesh cry out in sympathy with his ghastly wounds.

The crowd surged forward, spitting on him and striking him with whatever they could find. Butchery, that's what it was. The soldiers did nothing to stop them.

"Crucify him, crucify him."

Their screams forced the veins on their necks to pulsate and their faces to distort grotesquely. These were my fellow Jews insisting on this obscene punishment. How could they? Had they not seen hundreds of their countrymen agonizing on crosses littering the roadsides? Had they not hated the Romans for inflicting such cruelty? Why couldn't they call for stoning—the Jewish way—harsh, but much more swift than death on a cross? This person must be guilty of the most heinous crime imaginable for them to call down this despised Roman torture.

He fell, right in front of me. The crowd surged forward, kicking him, stomping on his defenseless body.

Why the soldiers pulled me from the mob I don't know.

"Help him up."

It was a gruff command, not a request. I struggled against his dead weight, against the pain I saw on his face. His body shuddered in twisted and tormented spasms when I touched his wounds.

"Put the crossbar on his back."

He fell again without a sound.

"You carry it."

Another command, this time with a sneering grin.

It was uphill now and he agonized with every step. The mob continued lashing out at him. I watched from behind as we struggled our way up the steep incline. The bloody beam across my shoulders stained my Passover clothes. My muscles ached.

That was not the worst. I was now unclean for having touched human blood and the instrument of torture. My Passover was ruined . . . *ruined*. My religious pilgrimage was for nothing.

Then—where it came from I don't know—that redeeming image of the first Passover in Egypt swept over me—the image of lamb's blood splashed on the lintels over the doors sparing my people from God's wrath—it came to me right here, in the midst of this hellish scene.

Was I witnessing a new *Exodus*—another escape from bondage?

Another sacrificial Lamb was staggering up the hill in front of me. I carried his blood on the 'lintel' stretched across my shoulders. Suddenly, I knew he was the spotless Lamb of God, the one Isaiah the prophet had predicted! I believed the revelation—my promised Messiah had to die! The scene in all its ugliness became transformed. I knew I must follow him to his place of undeserved death, a death that would set me free.

It was Passover Friday. The ugliness and brutality of the day— I saw it now—had a 'good' purpose, formed and designed from the beginning of time. The puzzling prophecies became clear to me. By his bleeding stripes dripping from the crossbeam lintel scarring my shoulders I would be redeemed, saved from the punishment I deserved, as I carried the cross of the Lamb of God who takes away the sins of the world.

Questions:

God placed Simon of Cyrene in that spot precisely for His purpose.
Have we found ourselves in similar situations where carrying someone else's 'cross' became an opportunity for witness?
How did we respond? How should we respond?

Scripture: Mary at the Foot of the Cross

And when they came to a place called Golgotha, they offered him wine to drink, mixed with gall, but when he tasted it he would not drink it.
And when they had crucified him, they divided his garments among them by casting lots. Then they sat down and kept watch over him there.
And over his head they put the charge against him, which read, "This is Jesus, the King of the Jews."
(Matthew 27: 33—38)

Pietá: Mary Speaks

Mary, the Mother of Jesus, *doesn't speak throughout the Passion narratives of the Gospels.*

We can only imagine what she may have said or thought as she witnessed the sacrifice of her Son. According to many traditions she journeyed to Ephesus and lived her remaining days in the Christian colony there, accompanied by John.

In this soliloquy her image is presented in the likeness of Michelangelo's early and familiar Pieta, *where her left hand is extended almost as if she is offering her son for the redemption of the world according to God's plan. She is revered as God's chosen 'vessel' for the birth of His Son by all wings of Christianity.*

I didn't speak.

If I had tried what could I say? I would fall apart before a single word hit the foul air of Golgotha. I want to be strong for him. All my spirit can muster is this outstretched left hand with my palm facing upwards toward him.

I'm not sure I know what the gesture means. It seems the only way to release the agony I feel for my dying, beloved son.

Some say it is a question:

"Why, why is this happening to my first-born?"

I know better. Before Jesus was born an angel told my husband this child would save his people from their sins. In my culture sins can only be covered by a blood sacrifice. I guess I have known my whole life that this child was for the world, come what may.

I remember—in the Temple—when he was dedicated to God, old Simeon said this child would create a sword-pierced path not only for my people, but to the Gentiles as well. Even in my confusion—I understood, and rejoiced in spite of my pain.

I remember my Bethlehem days and the prophet's warning of King Herod's plan:

A voice is heard in Rama, lamentation and bitter
weeping.
Rachel is weeping for her children;
she refuses to be comforted, because they are no more.
(Jeremiah 31: 15)

I dreaded the prophecy, praying,

"But please, Lord, don't take my child!
How could my innocent, nursing newborn's death fulfill
your promise?
Spare my son as you did Isaac of old."

My God heard my plea. We escaped Herod's wrath.

So, in truth, the gesture may be my way of saying,

"This is my son, God's Son,
an offering for the sins of the whole world."

My first prayer for deliverance those many years ago was answered; I dare not ask again. Though my heart breaks, I give him now for God's purposes.

Sometimes gestures are more powerful than words. I remain silent now in my sorrow. My up-raised hand speaks an eternal truth.

There had been pain at his beginning, and now there is pain at his ending. When my newborn baby Jesus was placed upon my breast all the pains of childbirth vanished. The Holy Spirit had brought promise into the world through me; that became my joy.

Now, once again, to my grief, Jeremiah's prophetic voice has descended upon this forsaken hill . . .

A voice is heard in Ramah . . . Rachel is weeping for
her children . . .
Rachel is weeping . . . Rachel . . .

The sword—that prophecy . . . that awful prophecy . . . I cannot escape: *I . . . am . . . Rachel!*

The pain I feel at the foot of the cross is different. It is deeper. Unfathomable. Unsearchable. Unquenchable. No mother should lose a child; it isn't the natural order of things. And when my son is delivered to me from the cross and lies across my bosom for the final time it will be the end of earthly joy for me—just as his birth was joy's beginning.

I believe—my whole life I have believed. I have not been silent for confusion; no—my silence is from certainty. God has a plan— I'm sure of it in spite of what I feel, shivering and tormented on this storm-tossed hill of crosses, shuddering at my beloved son's last breath. And so I will trust the God of Abraham, Isaac, and Jacob.

"ADONAI—ADONAI, take my tears and my lament.
Make of them a sacred song of deliverance—for my sake,
for your high purpose,
and for the promised salvation of Israel and the world."

Questions:

*Mary's prayers were not always answered in the way she would
have hoped, but she embraced the outcome as from God.
What is our response when it appears our prayers are not
answered in accordance with our desires?
Are we able to see God at work according to His plan even when
it is contrary to ours?*

DAY SIX

Crucifixion and Entombment

*The Centurion, Joseph of Arimathea,
and Mary Magdalene*

Scripture: The Centurion at the Foot of the Cross

*And when the sixth hour had come, darkness fell over the whole
land until the ninth hour . . . . And Jesus uttered a loud cry, and
breathed his last. And the veil of the temple was torn in two
from top to bottom.*
*And when the centurion, who was standing right in front of him,
saw the way he breathed his last, he said,
"Truly this man was the Son of God."*
(Mark 15:33, 37–39)

The Centurion Speaks

*Many traditions suggest the Centurion became a convert to Christianity and was martyred for his faith. Un-named in the Gospels,
he is later given the name Longinus (derived from the word for
'spear') in the apocryphal writings, the 'Gospel of Nicodemus', and
the 'Acts of Pilate'. The Centurion is considered a Saint in both the
Roman Catholic and Eastern Orthodox traditions. A monumental
sculpture by Bernini is fixed to one of the four great pillars holding
up the central structure and dome of St. Peter's Basilica in Rome. It
is given the title Longinus.*

*One legend has it that the Centurion suffered for having pierced
Jesus with a spear, and was condemned to live in a cave where he
would be mauled by a lion every night until the end of time.*

If you've seen one crucifixion, you've seen 'em all. It's always the same. Thieves, insurrectionists, murderers—they all get their just desserts. Good riddance!

I hate this dirty job. We wrestle the terrified lawbreaker to the ground, nail him to a cross, raise it, and drop it in a hole. The sudden impact rips their flesh as the body tears against the spikes. Their gut-wrenching screams fill the dusty air. You never get used to that sound, never.

Then you wait, sometimes for hours, until they die. You try to block out their curdling screams. The strongest of them push up with their legs to relieve the lungs from being suffocated by their collapsing ribcage. If the weather is bad, or we just get tired of waiting, we break their legs. No more pushing; death comes quickly.

It took years for me to rise to the position of Centurion. I served my time in some of the most dreary, god-forsaken outposts of the Empire, slowly advancing through the ranks. I looked forward to commanding a garrison of one hundred men. I was eager for the glamour of conquest—the triumphal march into Rome—receiving a hero's welcome from our Caesar. The thought of such future glories sustained me. I consoled myself,

"It will be worth it in the end."

But here I am in this Jewish wasteland, standing guard over the crucifixions of hundreds of zealots and criminals. It is the lowest duty in the military. Only Roman gravediggers are treated with more contempt. This is not what I signed up for.

On this hill they rightly call the 'place of the skull', the day started out the same as every other day. I said out loud, to no one in particular,

"Only three crucifixions today—less stressful."

Soon a large crowd gathered—that was unusual. Typically no one is there except for a few family members, and even they don't always show up. They were dressed in fine robes—that was unusual too.

"Must be the religious leaders from Jerusalem.
What are they doing here?"

Their leader began hurling insults at the man hanging in the middle; the others picked up the jeering.

The central figure had been brutalized far beyond the other two. His flayed skin hung in ribbons, his bones laid bare. Someone had jammed woven thorn branches on his head like an imitation crown. A sign was written and nailed to the upper post in languages I couldn't read. I've crucified hundreds of men—all of them scum of the earth—but never have I seen a body whipped like this! Who was this criminal?

The other two were dying, alone. One shouted obscenities at the figure in the middle,

"Are you not the Messiah? Save yourself and us!"

Save yourself? Impossible. The second responded in anger,

"Do you not even fear God . . . we are receiving what we
deserve for our deeds;
but this man has done nothing wrong . . . ."

Infuriated, I screamed against this insanity,

"Hurry up and die! I'm sick of this gibberish."

Then to my men,

"Break those complainer's legs; that will shut them up."

The next words came from the thief on the right.

"Jesus, remember me when you come into your kingdom."

Kingdom? It was crazy talk. No one ever survives crucifixion. They deserve to die! To hell with them!

Then the brutalized one spoke,

"Truly, today you shall be with me in paradise."

Was he delusional? At first I thought so.

Those words—*"Today . . . Paradise"*—stymied the taunts of the gathered crowd, and seemed to suck all the energy from the universe into a nucleus ready to explode. A clinging, cloying, saturating darkness fell heavy upon us—like a shroud. The ground shook violently.

The quaking earth and the blotted heavens wove another frightening counterpoint. The universe began howling, raging against the slaughter on this hill. The crowd scattered, screaming down the hill toward the city tripping over their sandals and robes. I ordered my terrified men:

"Stay in place—or die!"

Then—I swear I heard it: ripping, tearing sounds coming from the Jewish temple a great distance away. Louder and louder—*ripping—tearing*—it seemed it would never end. What is happening?

"Father, forgive them. They don't know what they are doing."

I caught my breath. Words swirled in my confused mind,

> *"Forgive them? What is this forgiveness?*
> *Two are dead, and the third is dying,*
> *They're destined for Hell, not Paradise!"*

Then, it sprang from a deep, hidden place inside—

"Forgive me? For what?"

Guilt had never entered my mind. I was trained to be brutal. I was paid to kill without remorse. My victims never forgave me for the torment I meted out to them; they pleaded with me to forgive *them*, hoping for a reprieve.

I began to wonder who I really was. At the same time I began to wonder who he was. My heart beat agonizingly against my breastplate; I could hear it above the churning, swirling wind. Then he uttered his final words . . .

"Father, into Thy hands I commend my spirit."

My next words came from nowhere. Silent at first, my transforming whisper began pushing against the darkness of my heart. Then rising. The heat of this involuntary testimony seared my throat:

> *"I accept your forgiveness.*
> *Grant me a future in your paradise."*

What was I saying?

Then my words mounted to a deafening roar, exploding beyond my comprehension, screaming above the fury of the rattling earth and the raging heavens. It was as if all the voices of creation had gathered into a shout coming just from me, tearing and unraveling the curtains of the shattered past and heralding the indestructible fabric of the future:

"Truly,"

I cried with astounding conviction,

"Truly this man was the Son of God!"

Questions:

What a revelation! What a transformation!
The centurion's view of death was that it was the final end of
a meaningless life—until this moment. He saw in the death of
Jesus something of promise,
something God-like.
In what ways do we see the sacrifice of Jesus and His resurrec-
tion as transformative?
Do our lives reflect that transformation? In other words, is the
difference between our 'before' and 'after' observable?

Scripture: Joseph of Arimathea Asks for the Body of Jesus

Later, Joseph of Arimathea asked Pilate for the body of Jesus.
Now Joseph was a disciple of Jesus, but secretly because he feared
the Jewish leaders. With Pilate's permission, he came and took
the body away. He was accompanied by Nicodemus, the man
who earlier had visited Jesus at night At the place where Jesus
was crucified, there was a garden, and in the garden a new
tomb, in which no one had ever been laid.
(John 19: 38—42)

Joseph of Arimathea considers 'The Christ'

Joseph of Arimathea *appears in all four Gospels, and is also mentioned*
in many apocryphal and non-canonical accounts. He and Nicodemus
appear at the crucifixion and are depicted in countless works of art
removing Jesus' body from the cross. His tomb became the burial place
for Jesus after his crucifixion. It is thought by some that he bore witness
of Jesus' resurrection to Caiaphas, the High Priest.

Legend suggests he became the first Bishop of the British Isles.
In the 12th century he was connected to the 'Arthurian Cycle' as the
first keeper of the Holy Grail. Joseph of Arimathea is revered as a
Saint in the Roman Catholic and Eastern Orthodox traditions.

Nicodemus does not appear in the Synoptic Gospels, but is
mentioned in detail three times in the Gospel of John. He may be

the same Nicodemus mentioned in the Talmud as a wealthy holy man reputed to have miraculous powers. Nicodemus is shown with Joseph of Arimathea in countless paintings of the deposition of Jesus from the cross.

According to tradition, Nicodemus heeded the invitation of Jesus, became a follower, and was martyred for his faith. He is revered as a Saint by various Orthodox traditions as well as the Roman Catholic Church.

My name is Joseph. I am a secret follower of Jesus from the village of Arimathea. The prophet Samuel was born there. Samuel—*who heard the voice of God!* Breaking with birthrights and tradition he chose David the shepherd boy and youngest of his brothers to be king of Israel. His divinely inspired choice ran counter to the rights of inheritance. They say Messiah will come from the Davidic line.

The story of Samuel and David was a great inspiration to me. I prayed that I too would be used of God. I wanted to see the divine purpose in life, not the human. I longed to be like Samuel! I wanted to hear the voice of God!

I dedicated my life to Him, and became a Pharisee.

I knew all the controversies swirling around the man from Nazareth, how they say he was a threat to our traditions. The court of the Sanhedrin, of which I am a proud and prominent member, was determined to find ways to end what they called his heretical teaching.

But . . . there was something about his manner, his teaching that was compelling to me; it rang true. Yes, his talk about 'rising from the dead' was confusing. The way we Pharisees see it, resurrection is for all believers at the end of time, not for one man in the middle of time. Certainly not for Messiah; Messiah doesn't die. His words caused me to search my Scriptures in ways I never considered before. What have I missed? What did the prophets really say about Messiah? And I thought,

*"What would my hero Samuel do if confronted by this
most unlikely man of peace,
this miracle worker with new ideas about resurrection?"*

It was dangerous to be one of the Nazarene's followers. I sought ways to be near him without being detected. I hid in the shadows, hearing his words at a distance.

I was not alone. There was Nicodemus, a fellow from the Sanhedrin and a great teacher of the Law. Like me, he witnessed the crowds gathering around Jesus. Like me, he thought there was great power embedded in the carpenter's teaching; it had weight. Jesus was answering questions that had plagued him for years. It was, Nicodemus said,

" . . . of God."

Our fellow Pharisees tried to debunk the Nazarene's teaching. Not Nicodemus. He made a secret visit to Jesus under the cover of night:

*"Rabbi, we know you are a teacher who has come from
God. For no one could do the miraculous signs that you
do unless God were with him."*
(John 3:2)

Then Nicodemus, one of our greatest teachers, asked the peasant from Nazareth how he could be assured of Heaven—Nicodemus, of all people! One of our most learned and respected religious leaders! As a Pharisee he had observed all the Laws, lived an upright life, studied the Scriptures—if anyone should be assured of Heaven it was him. But Jesus' reply left him speechless and confounded:

"You must be born again."

Return to his mother's womb? How was that possible? He struggled to understand while continuing his pursuit of him.

I, too, was convinced a new spiritual path was forming through this astounding teacher. I became increasingly bold in the council of the Sanhedrin, attempting to defend Jesus without divulging my allegiance.

The Sanhedrin's heated and angry rhetoric became a plan of action to do away with him. I had no choice but to speak up more strongly in his defense.

My reputation suffered. I was rebuked. I was ostracized, along with Nicodemus.

Our leaders acted swiftly. Jesus was captured—on Passover night, no less! Can you imagine such a grave insult to our sacred feast?

The next hours were filled with horror. We stood aside, the two of us, and witnessed the flogging and shredding of his body. We joined the procession to the crucifixion as silent mourners even as the mob raged around us. Satisfied with what they had accomplished, the chief priests followed him to Golgotha forging a trail of smug arrogance. We stood on the hill of condemnation lamenting the indescribable insults circling the one we had hoped was our promised Messiah.

"Into Thy hands I commit my spirit."

He died there, surrounded by a howling mob, a howling wind, and an unearthly ripping sound in the distance. Outraged, we asked each other,

"How can a good man be put to death?"

Then, more from utter confusion than outrage, we asked,

"How can Messiah—if he is Messiah—how can Messiah die?"

We were ashamed of our membership on the court. Men of God? I used to think so. No longer. What now?

We went to Pilate. I asked for Jesus' body. We carried it to the tomb I had intended for myself. As if it wasn't enough to be 'outcasts' from the Sanhedrin, we were now condemned by Mosaic Law for touching a corpse. It no longer mattered.

The words of our prophet Isaiah came clear:

He was assigned a grave with the wicked, and with the
rich in his death, though he had done no violence, nor
was any deceit in his mouth.
(Isaiah 53:9)

Was he talking about Jesus? Were we part of the prophecy? Were we part of God's plan?

We have nothing left but to wait for the 'end time', for the resurrection of the dead—for our own resurrection.

Leaving the sealed tomb and the Roman guards behind, my last thought was of Samuel. What did he know about the unsung David when he heeded God's command? Did he know that his unlikely choice was God's chosen, heaven-sent path to Messiah?

And what did we know, Nicodemus and me, about our unsung Nazarene? Did we know whether our sympathies for this righteous man would be validated? Would he, like Job, be vindicated? Would his 'Third Day' predictions fulfill Isaiah's elusive prophecies?

Oh, to be a modern day Samuel! If only my faith in this man Jesus can overcome my doubt; if only I live to witness the kingly enthronement of this son of David, our friend, the one I hope is our promised Deliverer—our Messiah!

Questions:

Joseph of Arimathea and Nicodemus lived lives of righteousness
and good works, yet they saw something greater in the teaching
of Jesus, and desired it,
risking their lives and reputations in the process.
They sought a divine purpose in life.
What is our divine calling beyond living a good and upright life?
How can we embrace Christ's example?
Would we risk our lives and reputation for it?

Scripture: Mary Magdalene at the Tomb of Jesus

Mary Magdalene and the other Mary were looking on to see where he was laid.
(Mark 15:47)

Mary Magdalene Speaks

Mary Magdalene, *mentioned twelve times in the Gospels, was present at both the crucifixion and resurrection of Jesus. Because she was the first to realize Jesus had been raised from the dead, and was the first to declare it to the others, she is often called the 'apostle to the Apostles'. After reporting the resurrection of Jesus she disappears from Scripture, though she is mentioned in various Apocryphal accounts and the Gnostic Gospels.*

One legend says she lived as a hermit in a cave for the last thirty years of her life. The Orthodox tradition says she lived with Mary, the mother of Jesus, in Ephesus.

Mary Magdalene is revered as a Saint in many major Christian religious traditions.

Her two monologues in 'Silent Voices' are infused with the drama of 'sounds': condemnation, pounding, darkness, light, birds of the night and morning, and finally invitation.

I was there—in Pilate's courtyard. Those sounds! The flogging! The death sentence! I heard them—me, the wild-eyed and cringing woman from Magdala, the one possessed by seven demons. But demonic torment was nothing compared to those condemning words:

"Crucify him, crucify him."

My Savior! The one who didn't shun me when all others did! The one who released me from my demonic prison! They still ring in my ears, those words.

I was there—at the cross—his mother and I, and young John. I held them close. I had to be their tower of strength, their citadel of compassion; it was bred into me by my circumstances and the choice of my name:

Magdala: 'A tower, a castle'.

I was strong for them, choking back my own sorrow while he sorrowed for *us*, his blood being poured out like a Passover substitute. He said as much yesterday.

"This is my blood . . . shed for you . . . ."

None of us understood those Passover words—until now.

Those aching sounds! The curses. The taunting. The cracking earth groaning in sympathy with his brokenness. Above all, the wind.

The wind! What was it I heard as the wind swirled around us in pitiable lament; it was as if the whole of nature suffered with him on that tree. I dare not repeat the dirge; it was too terrible. Once in history is enough.

I was the last to leave, hoping against hope it was just a bad dream. It wasn't.

I was there when they laid him in Joseph's tomb. The sounds of whips and nails, of staccato hammering, of mocking and jeering, of John's boyish sobs and Mary's throbbing heartache—all mingled with the agonizing sound of stone grinding against stone.

A sealing. A finality. Through the crashing hours of the sun's absence and a moonless sky, through the languid hours of the tortuous night those sounds tumbled over and over again in my heart. If ever there was a tuneless melody, this was such an elegy.

How could the one who rescued me from my demons be dead? Oh, how I had hoped! How I had believed—only to be invaded by another debilitating demon—the demon of disbelief, the demon of doubt. The others were right, I regrettably confessed. He wasn't who we thought he was. I wept as I wrestled in vain with my betrayal of faith.

Questions:

Mary Magdalene, like all those who followed Jesus, had hoped he was Messiah. Nothing in their understanding of Scripture had prepared them for a dying Messiah, much less one who would then be raised.
The death of Jesus destroyed her hope and gave rise to overwhelming doubt.
Death is our enemy and doubt leads to a death-like existence. How can we describe the resurrection we hope for, and the resurrected life we profess?
Has faith truly overcome our occasional tendencies to doubt?

DAY SEVEN

Sunday

The Roman Guard, Mary Magdalene, and the Emmaus Road Appearance of Christ

Scripture: The Tomb is Made Secure

The chief priests and the Pharisees gathered together with Pilate, and said, "Sir, we remember that when he was still alive that deceiver said,
'After three days I am to rise again.' Therefore, give orders for the grave to be made secure until the third day, lest the disciples come and steal him away and say to the people, 'He has risen from the dead'" . . .
Pilate said to them, "You have a guard." And they went and made the grave secure, and set a seal on the stone.
(Matthew 27:62–66; 28:2–4)

A Roman Guard Speaks

There may or may not have been a Roman Guard at the Tomb. It is unclear how to interpret the words in Scripture, "You have a guard," when such a force was requested. It can be interpreted with emphasis on the word 'you', suggesting the Jewish leaders had their own Temple Guards and were told to use them. It can also be interpreted as indicating that the request for a Roman Guard was granted. Either way there was a guard at the tomb consisting of more than one person. Because it was Passover the thought is that no Jewish guard would be given an assignment that called for the use of weapons.

The Roman Guard was constituted as is characterized in the 'Silent Voices' soliloquy. There are no other legends or traditions that came into existence surrounding those who guarded the tomb.

_____

There had been rumors. We were prepared. There would be no conspiracy to steal *this* body. It took all of us to roll that two-ton stone across the mouth of the tomb. The stone itself was a deterrent; the Roman seal even more so. Anyone disturbing that official sign would die swiftly.

Then, of course, there was our presence—sixteen of us lined up in front of the tomb in four ranks of four. It was the typical Roman Guard. We wore armor, and our plumed helmets made us look even taller and more imposing than we were. We each carried a shield, a sword, and a spear. The crack troops of Rome, that's who we were. Only a fool would dare confront us.

We had orders. The four in front of the tomb were on alert; the other twelve could rest. Every hour we changed positions, insuring that a fresh group of four always guarded the grave.

If any one of the four assigned to be alert were to fall asleep all sixteen of us would be put to death. That's the rule; that's the order. You can be sure we kept our eyes on each other as well as on the tomb!

In truth, we didn't expect any disturbance. The Nazarene's followers ran away when we arrested him. Even the betrayer hanged himself. Cowards! There had been no report of any of them since Friday. They probably were hiding somewhere for fear of their lives, or else they had escaped Jerusalem and were headed north. Either way, our job was easy. With or without a guard it was a safe bet the tomb would be unchallenged. But . . . just to be safe . . . those rumors, you know.

Through the night of Friday, through the long, tedious hours of Saturday and into the night, we kept our hourly carousel of guards. No one had approached anywhere near the tomb. We were bored, and consumed by thoughts of returning to our families in Rome.

Then . . . what is this? Darkness! Darker-than-night, suffocating darkness!

Scripture: The Earthquake

And behold, a severe earthquake had occurred, for an angel of the Lord descended from heaven and came and rolled away the stone and sat upon it.
And his appearance was like lightning, and his garment as white as snow; and the guards shook for fear of him, and became like dead men.
(Matthew 27:62–66; 28:2–4)

The Roman Guard Speaks Again

Darkness! Darker-than-night, suffocating darkness!

There was a sound like thunder, but without clouds or rain. Puzzling at first; then it became deafening. It roared, and our shouts of alarm were drowned in the cataclysm. The ground began to tremble, slowly growing through a rapid and turbulent crescendo into violent shaking. It became impossible to stand. We collapsed in fear.

In our clouded sight all of nature seemed to shift on its axis. Meridians seemed altered. Earth's gyro was careening out of control. Orientations appeared irreconcilable with history. We clung to our convulsing world crying to our gods,

"Make it return to normal!"

No answer.

That giant stone began to move away from the tomb with an ear-splitting, cracking sound, exposing the grave itself. What potential horror of decay lurked inside? We trembled at the thought.

Light! How can I describe it—a brilliant, blinding light pierced the darkness and enveloped the stone. It was as if the thunder had produced lightening—but . . . wait . . . that would have reversed nature's order! And the lightening was not a flash, but a penetrating incandescence, as if the bolt itself was eternal.

It wasn't lightening at all! It was in appearance like a man, but in essence like a god. Arrayed in robes of dazzling white—whiter than any description, beyond comprehension, like color re-gathered into the prism preceding the first cosmic explosion. The apparition gestured triumphantly toward the emptiness the stone had uncovered. I was hesitant to look, but did, expecting to be re-pulsed by the sight. Where was the utter blackness of this pathway to death—where was the mutilated body I had seen entombed two short days ago?

Shadows began spinning—nature's order *was* being re-versed—back, back—unmasking the evolution of the world bit by bit, shredding ideas and philosophies. Back toward foundations, ancient creeds, systems and stratagems—back through the Babel of language, back through the origination of firmament and stars, the creation of the gods themselves—discarding all invention, all genius, disintegrating all of history, all that one had imagined of existence—back and back, until there was but one solitary being alone in the nascent universe. I struggled to give it a name—

"The Beginner of All Things Seen and Unseen."

The *Beginner* revealed himself—he was a *Living Presence* standing upright against the empty stone slab, not moving, yet filling every void in creation. Burnished radiance. Heat. Energy. Burning brighter than a thousand suns, rendering the apparition on the stone pale by comparison. No armaments, no machines of war, no valor, no bravery, not ten thousand armies or an accumu-lation of the world's greatest empires could ever stand against the light of that *Living Presence*.

Crimson flames spun from his hands and feet, beckoning my scarlet world. A deeper crimson sprang from his side, a spot once wounded—was it an invitation?

"Come now, and let us reason together," says the Lord.
"Though your sins are as scarlet, they will be white as
snow."
(Isaiah 1:18)

I was peering into a new dimension. Should I embrace it or flee from it in terror like the others? I lay there alone, naked of all pretense, ignorant of fear, immune to trembling, held captive by a blind and dumb neutrality. I could not escape those crimson flames, nor could I embrace them.

As a Roman, I did not believe in hell and there was no heaven—just life and the void called death. I was trapped—caught between mind and heart. My heart wanted what the *Living Presence* offered, but my mind doubted my need to want. My heart wanted what I saw of divinity, yet my mind felt reluctant to part with my humanity. The two forces—negative mind and positive heart—fought within me. As a Roman guard I foolishly allowed the one I had always lived by to reign—that hellish force of mind— narrowing my choices, obliterating all hope.

If I fled I would die in Pilate's court for dereliction of duty; if I stayed I would most certainly die in the all-consuming light of that *Living Presence.* I was a dead man regardless.

I made my decisive and destructive choice: I ran. I ran for my life. I, one of the crack troops of Rome, fled in utter, unfettered, uncontrolled terror. I refused the crimson invitation!

I chose my scarlet sepulcher over his 'white as snow' paradise!

Questions:

The Soldier at the tomb was the only person who saw the actual resurrection, yet he felt trapped between 'reason' and 'faith'. What he saw was beyond reasonable, rational explanation. All the natural laws (God's laws) were being reversed: 2nd Law of

Thermodynamics—that all things move from order to chaos, integration to disintegration, life to death—was being thwarted. Yet he refused to embrace the incredible event he witnessed.
Hard to believe!
How many times have we refused to acknowledge what we know to be true, yet cannot explain? In our world consumed by scientific 'provability', do we truly 'live by faith and not by rational sight'?

Scripture: Mary Magdalene Visits the Empty Tomb

*Now on the first day of the week Mary Magdalene came early
to the tomb, while it was still dark, and saw the stone already
taken away from the tomb . . . . She turned around, and beheld
Jesus standing there, and did not know that it was Jesus . . . .
Jesus said to her, "Mary!" She turned and said to him in Hebrew,
"Rabboni!"
(John 20:1–16)*

Mary Magdalene Speaks Again

They continued throughout the bleak night of my despair, those
sounds of whips and nails, and staccato hammering. They continued, those sounds of mocking and jeering, of John's boyish sobs
and Mary's throbbing heartache—all mingled with the agonizing
sound of stone grinding against stone.

I awoke early Sunday, compelled by those awful sounds to go
back to the tomb. A nightingale was singing in the dark attempting to cheer its own solitude. I desired that same song for my own
loneliness. The sounds moved me, softening my despair, though I
knew not why.

The stone lay aside! The tomb was empty! I felt an eruption
of rage. I cried out,

*"What have they done with his body?
Wasn't it enough to kill him?*

I sought equilibrium for my despair. What to do? I ran to Peter and John. They ran to the tomb and left without a word; only the lament of the nightingale lingered as the darkness diminished.

Those sounds became visions! Visions became Angels! Angels began singing vibrant songs like those I never dreamt to hear—beyond our human spectrum!

"He is not here, but has risen just as he said."

Then another sound. It was the song of the morning Lark, with a beauty overcoming the sad and sullen lament of the nightingale, transposing it into hymns of eternity. It melodied a spiritual daybreak. It sang—even before the created sun broke the thin line marking the advent from night to day. At that moment earth and heaven became one. Then I remembered his words:

"A little while, and you will no longer behold me;
and again a little while, and you will see me."
(John 16:16)

Immediately I heard it; not the consoling nightingale; not the Lark hinting at the dawn.

Another sound!

It came to me across the desolate garden, beyond the silent tombs—a faint, gentle, compelling voice that cancelled out the final demon of my soul . . .

"Mary."
"Rabboni!"

Question:

Have we, like the Magdalene, heard His voice and reverently embraced it?

86

Scripture: The Disciples on the Emmaus Road

And behold, two of them were going that very day to a village named Emmaus . . . . And it came about that while they were conversing and discussing, Jesus himself approached, and began traveling with them. But their eyes were prevented from recognizing him . . . . And beginning with Moses and with all the prophets [Jesus] explained to them the things concerning himself in all the Scriptures . . . . When he reclined at the table with them, he took the bread and blessed it, and breaking it, he began giving it to them. And their eyes were opened . . . .

(Luke 24)

Cleopas and His Friend Speak

Cleopas and his Friend *are mentioned in only one Gospel account, Luke 24. John's Gospel mentions a Clopas or a Cleophas, and some believe they are the same person who walked the road to Emmaus. While not one of the 'twelve', it is thought Cleopas was a close follower of Jesus; his name appears on several lists of the Seventy Disciples appointed and sent out by Jesus. He is mentioned as succeeding James, the brother of Jesus, as Bishop of Jerusalem.*

According to Eusebius, quoting Hegesippus (writing in 180 AD), Cleopas was the brother of Mary's husband Joseph. Some suggest his un-named companion was the Gospel writer Luke.

In the Orthodox tradition the companion is thought to be Alexander, one of the sons of Simon of Cyrene.

We had to make a run for it—get out before we were discovered. Since Thursday night we had been hiding, waiting for a chance to escape Jerusalem. Everything was falling apart. Peter was trying to disassociate himself from Jesus. Judas, the betrayer, hanged himself. The rest of us huddled together in the darkness of a small room weeping, searching for answers, singing Psalms of profound lament.

Before dawn the two of us left via the deserted side streets heading toward the Jaffa Gate. It was risky, as the portal was often locked to keep out marauders, hyenas and jackals. Being the most hated and feared gate it also was the most promising for our getaway; it should be deserted precisely because it is hated and feared.

We were in luck! The gate was open; no one was on duty.

Outside the Jaffa gate the despicable garbage pit stared us in the face. We could smell the blazing sulfur.

The air was filled with acrid smoke and haunted memories of Israel's ancient apostasy: generations of sons and daughters thrown into the fires, sacrificed to Moloch and Baal. It was Gehenna! Hell!

We had just been through a different hell these last few days; another gruesome sacrifice, another gut-wrenching apostasy, another son crucified to the godless pride of our chief priests. Though we dreaded the path through Gehenna it was our only choice if we were to survive.

We exited the gate and descended into the abyss.

One more journey through hell in order to escape another hell couldn't be any worse than what we had already experienced.

We hurried northwest toward our small village, about seven miles away. If we could make it to Emmaus without being discovered our lives might return to normal. It was slow going. Every time we saw anyone we fled the dusty path and hid in the underbrush. The further we walked, the fewer people we saw. We finally were in the clear and simply stayed on the road.

He came out of nowhere. We didn't see him approach—he was just there walking beside us!

We didn't recognize the stranger; we had other things on our minds—like survival.

You know what they say: 'You see what you expect to see.'

I suppose you could also say: 'You don't see what you don't expect to see'.

**"What are you discussing with each other?
Why are you so downcast?"**

What a question! Who wouldn't be, after what we'd been through. Everyone knew what had been happening in Jerusalem. Why not him?

We told him what had happened to our friend, lamenting the events following Passover.

We had hoped,

We said it in unison . . .

We had hoped he was Israel's Messiah.

Had hoped—past tense! There! We finally admitted it. Over. Dashed dreams. Devastation!

Then, strangely, and for a purpose we couldn't fathom, he began talking about Israel's prophets.

**How foolish you are, and how slow of heart to believe
all that the prophets have declared!
(Luke 24:25)**

He knew our scriptures like a Rabbi, but his interpretations were confounding! He built his religious premise prophetic voice by prophetic voice, finally arriving at the apex of his argument. When he kept saying,

According to the Scriptures . . .

—not 'according to the Rabbis'—he seemed to be speaking from a higher authority.

**Was it not necessary that the Messiah should suffer
these things**

and then enter into his glory?
(Luke 24:26)

He said the Son of Man was ordained to die 'according to the scriptures'. It was God's plan, 'according to the scriptures'.

Ordained to die? God's plan? According to the scriptures? Not according to any account we ever heard before.

How can all our teachers be wrong? He continued his attempts to persuade us.

This conversation—the intensity of it— at first beyond our ability to comprehend—was beginning to make sense. Cleopas and I looked at each other and silently mouthed,

Who is this stranger?

He invited us to share a simple meal with him: bread and wine—they appeared out of nowhere just as he had. We welcomed the respite. Our brains were about to explode.

Those mind-shattering views of our prophets . . .

. . . and in addition—we were exhausted from our three-day ordeal.

Wait—has it been three days? Cleopas, what day is it?

Sunday.

No. What day is it? I mean, is it the first, second, or third since our friend was crucified and we went into hiding?

Third. It's the third day.
Yes. It's the third day.

Slowly it began to register in our confused minds; our friend had always talked about the 'third day'.

I will be killed . . . but on the third day . . . on the third day . . .

What was it that was supposed to happen on the 'third day'?
The stranger took bread, broke it, and gave it to us. Could it be; could it possibly be him?

We flashed back to the miraculous feeding of the five thousand. We had seen it with our own eyes!

Were we experiencing a new miraculous feeding?

The way he held it.

The way he blessed it.

Just like Thursday in the Upper Room! He's alive! We shouted it together,

You're alive!

We ran in wild circles.

Jumping up and down.

Bumping into walls.

Losing our sandals as well as our balance.

Losing our minds in joy, tumbling to the ground in gales of tearful laughter.

Jesus is alive! Jesus is alive!

Over and over again.

Jesus is alive! Jesus is alive!

It came back to us; he had said he would suffer and die, 'But on the third day . . . be raised!' It wasn't one of his parables—it was literally true!

We dropped everything and began running back up the road toward the city we had abandoned in fear just hours before. Back we raced, through the dreaded Valley of Gehenna, the valley of sacrifice, the valley of hell. We had to descend once again into that hell in order to come at last to Jerusalem—a new Jerusalem.

Back through the valley of the shadow of death and hell toward a new 'resurrected life'.

Wait . . . what did you just say? The shadow of Death? Hell? Life?

Then it struck us like a hammerblow: Jesus had taken the same journey!

Questions:

The poet Elizabeth Barrett Browning, reflecting on Moses'
encounter with the burning bush, wrote:
"Earth's crammed with heaven,
And every common bush afire with God;
But only he who sees takes off his shoes . . . "
Medieval Christians believed they were surrounded by daily
miracles.
They saw them because they were looking for them.
Are we looking?
The appearance of the risen Christ on the Emmaus Road was a
miracle of God working beyond their understanding.
Are we open to such events in our commonplace world?
In how many ways have we felt God walking alongside us in our
everyday lives?
Can we recall times when we were confronted by 'a common
bush afire with God'?

DAY EIGHT

The Risen Christ Appears in the Upper Room

Doubt and Faith

Scripture: The Upper Room, Evening of the Third Day

That same hour they got up and returned to Jerusalem;
and they found the eleven and their companions gathered
together
They were saying, "The Lord has risen indeed . . . ."
Then they told what had happened on the road,
and how he had been made known to them
in the breaking of bread.
(Luke 24:33–35)
The Upper Room: Doubt and Faith
The upper room was a labyrinth of confusion.
It oozed with fear and reeked of doubt.
They had thought he was their Messiah!
Their dreams of God's kingdom being established?
Gone. Crucified.

"They were right; we were foolish to leave our fishing nets. If only we had listened to them we wouldn't be in this mess."

"Was he just another zealot?"

"Those miracles? Were they the work of a conjurer?"

"It doesn't matter. He's dead. Whatever he did, whoever he was, it's too late to think about it. We've got to get out of here. If they find us we'll suffer the same torture. Think! Think!! How do we escape?"

I stood up.

Someone had to arrest our downward spiral, so I attempted to impose a more rational outlook on our dilemma. We had to return to the time before Jesus entered our hearts, before we left our fishing nets, back to the days when the Messianic kingdom was a distant and future hope. Given my own grief, the attempt was challenging.

"Doubt is natural," *I said.*

I wanted to say that doubt is rational, but it was clear no one would think so; not in our irrational state. Doubt often springs up spontaneously when one is first confronted by failure, but I didn't think it wise to mention that either.

Failure was the last thing we wanted to admit.

"But . . . I . . . I can't stop thinking about him. We were so sure."

I said it again, louder this time:

"Doubt is natural. It's faith that's unnatural!"

It needed to be said. We had possessed faith, but where had it gotten us?

Here is a sad truth: the less an event has occurred in the past the more faith it takes to believe it will occur in the future—and the less it has occurred in the past the more likely it is it won't occur at all. So if an event has never occurred before, any faith that it will is misplaced, misguided.

I spoke again:

"Faith takes . . . faith, but it's hard to cling to it if we haven't experienced some previous foundation to hang our hopes on. To eliminate doubt, faith needs a track record. We don't have faith in Jesus' words about being raised on the third day because, first, we didn't understand what he meant—Messiah doesn't die—and second, there was no track record."

"Then how can faith be faith if we need evidence, this track record you keep talking about?"

Good question! I didn't have an answer.

In light of our shattered hopes the reality of death seemed far more persuasive than faith in a resurrection.

I tried again:

"We move through our lives knowing that all things end in death.

It's nature's way—God's way; it's built into creation itself.
Death doesn't take faith; it has a 'track record.'"

"So, are you saying that when we're born we immediately be-
gin the process of dying?"

"It's a morbid thought, I know, but it's true. Death is inevitable.
Whether or not we are always conscious of that fact, in our darkest moments we grapple with the truth of it."

They agreed, but the thought needed further embellishment:
"Yes, we live each day as if we'll live forever, but deep down we
know the real outcome. To doubt our life's sad conclusion is to
defy the natural order of things."

It was important to emphasize the 'natural order of things'.
We had to return to reality if we were going to survive.

"So you're saying Jesus' death should not have surprised us. It was
the un-timely brutality of it—that was the surprise."

"And we know you keep reminding us that he kept talking about
'rising on the third day', but who among us thought he meant it
literally? You? You? Don't you remember how we asked each other
what he was saying, but were afraid to ask *him*?"

"He's right! To think he meant 'rising' literally would have been
irrational, and he was nothing if not rational. It had to be a parable.
We all said it."

Agreement was growing in the room.
I continued, building the case that doubt was the only justifiable
response to the events of the last three days.

"Let me say it again. If Jesus was only a man he was destined to
die like the rest of us—which he did. If he was the Messiah then
he would have lived forever, never dying, not even once.
That's how we understand our scriptures and our Rabbis:
Messiah doesn't die; he comes to establish His kingdom."

"But those miracles?"

"Yes, I know, I know—Jesus could do miraculous things; and yes,
he taught us *about* the coming Kingdom.
But he died, so he couldn't possibly *be* the Kingdom.

His death proved he was just a man . . . a good man, but just a man."

I ended by inserting my capstone argument:
"If we had considered his words about rising from the dead to be actual, and literal—not a parable—we would most certainly have doubted him long before this. One must doubt claims that stand against God's laws of nature—that all things are born and die. Sad though it is, our doubts are justified."

So here we were, gathered in fear three days after he was crucified. Our fear had a triple focus: our friend's gruesome death, the loss of his 'kingdom promise', and above all the threat of our own crucifixions. While we had wanted his 'eternal presence', his death confirmed that the laws of creation remained undisturbed. Messiah? Not him, regretfully. We must wait for another—that is, if we survive.

(The women, having left to anoint his body, barged into the room.)

"He's alive!"
"We've seen him!"

They screamed it over and over again to each of us in turn, circling the room.
In spite of having made our tenuous peace with his death as well as our own doubts, the women's words set the room ablaze once more, but not for long.
Wishful thinking soon gave way to reality.
While the women continued their 'silly tale', the men scoffed.
The roaring interchanges with the women stopped as quickly as they had risen.
Confusion gave way to a gloomy silence.
Then another Interruption!
Cleopas and his companion, out of breath and trembling, burst through the door.
They had left early that morning to escape Jerusalem.
Why would they come back?
Their words tumbled in a rapid staccato:

"You won't believe this! We've seen Jesus!"

The women nodded vigorously.

"Our Jesus is alive!"

"He just appeared out of nowhere!"

"We actually talked with him."

Something about 'breaking bread' with Jesus, they said.

"We ate with him!"

I rose up in dissent, trying to quell their foolishness before it took root, shouting, "They must be having an apparent hallucination. Grief can do that."

"I'm telling you, we've seen him!"

We were becoming conflicted once again. Two reports. Women first—now men. But . . . we all said to reassure our certainty . . . no one comes back from the dead! Hope and blind faith were not enough to persuade us. Once again I argued, "Of course we want to believe your report, but doubt is the more reliable response. Emotions are misleading and we have to set them aside. If we continue to wallow in false hope, in un-natural faith, and in these apparent hallucinations, then we are all doomed."

"I agree. Someone has to put together an escape plan."

Cleopas, his friend, and the women screamed together:

"Listen to us! We're telling you the truth! We've seen . . . "

Their words were interrupted by an otherworldly stillness— no movement in the room or in the heavens— a momentary pause in the flow of time— a halt in the anticipation of their next breath— a vacuum waiting to be filled— an intrusive infusion of expectancy. In that instant, in the split second of eternity, Jesus appeared in the center of the room!

He just . . . appeared!

"No! Not another hallucination! Not us too!"

We fought against the appearance with all the doubt and rational-
ity we could muster.
But this time doubt and rationality weren't enough.

"Ghosts don't have bodies; he does!"

We were astonished; how could flesh and blood and physical com-
position penetrate locked doors and solid walls?
What kind of body was this?

"Ghosts don't have wounds; his are visible and crimson!"

We could see the fresh nail prints, yet they appeared completely
healed.
Then we remembered the long forgotten ancient text:
'He was wounded for our transgressions,
he was bruised for our iniquities,
the chastisement for our peace was upon him,
and by his stripes we are healed.'
(Isaiah 53: 5)
Had Isaiah foretold the suffering of Messiah?
Was this prophecy fulfilled in Jesus?
Then he spoke,
"I'm hungry. Have you anything here to eat?"

"Ghosts don't get hungry; he is!"
We gave him a piece of a broiled fish; he took it and ate it.
"He eats real food: not symbolic—real! Real!"
"Can it be; can it possibly be him?"

We flashed back to the miraculous feeding of the five thousand:
five small loaves and two fish—multiplied. We had seen it with our
own eyes!
We had eaten our fill, and gathered the baskets of abundance!
Were we experiencing a new miraculous feeding?
Were we witnessing a multiplication of faith?

"We see him. We touch him! He returns the touch."

"He breathes, and his chest rises and falls as he does!"

"He is three-dimensional. He has weight and volume, displacing air. He occupies space and moves around in it!"

At that very moment we erupted with unbridled joy—an 'I can't believe it' kind of joy, fully believing even as we said it. Jesus had been alive. He had died. He was alive again—resurrected! Our faith was being built upon a vibrant, pulsating new reality. We shouted it over and over again,

"He is the substance of things hoped for; the evidence of things not seen!"

Substance—evidence were suddenly unleashed in our presence, strangling the doubts that had strangled our faith. His body standing among us was the substance of what we had hoped for, even in our darkest moments of doubt. His actual, living, resurrected presence was the evidence filling the void of what we had not been able to see. Isn't that what faith is? Isn't that faith's reward?

"We don't need to live by metaphor any longer!"

"Eternal death is abolished! The prophecies are fulfilled!"

"Resurrection is real!"

"Precedent is established!"

"Doubt has died!"

"Faith is reborn!"

We shouted it in unison, brimming with faith and certainty:
"The Third Day; the Third Day!
Nothing will ever be the same again because of the 'Third Day'!"
"He is risen; he is risen indeed!"

Questions:

For three years the disciples saw the miracles of Jesus and heard him speak of his coming death and resurrection. Yet, when he died, they became confused and filled with doubts. For us, as it was for them, doubt is a natural response when questions arise or failure is encountered.

The battle between doubt and faith is the ultimate and most critical dilemma we face; we confront it in many circumstances of life. However, we know the antidote to doubt is found in the sacrifice and resurrection of Jesus.

The final questions are: Do we truly believe? Has our faith triumphed?

How does one live life with resurrection certainty? What does it look like?

About the Author

GREGORY S. ATHNOS
Emeritus Professor of Music
North Park University, Chicago, Illinois

GREGORY S. ATHNOS served as Associate Professor of Music for 32 years on the North Park University faculty. In his second year he founded the popular Chamber Singers and toured extensively with them throughout the United States, Canada, Scandinavia, and Italy. In 1975 he was founder and first conductor of the University Orchestra, continuing in that position until 1982. In 1986 he was appointed conductor of the University Choir, and led that organization in concert tours across the United States, Poland, Hungary, Sweden, Russia and Estonia. In 1993 he was guest conductor for the Chamber Orchestra of Pushkin, Russia, and the State Symphony of Estonia, conducting their first performances of Handel's *Messiah* since the Bolshevik Revolution in 1918.

The Majesty Chorale, under his leadership, was invited to participate in the 2008 pre-Olympic Festival in China. Most of the singers were Chinese-born Christians. They sang nine concerts of Sacred Music in Beijing, Tsingdao, and Shanghai.

Mr. Athnos was one of the most respected teachers on the University campus. 'Innovative', 'enthusiastic', 'provocative', and 'challenging' were terms often used by his students, who called his lectures 'lessons in life'. He also teaches in the national Elderhostel/Road Scholar program on two campuses, Wisconsin and New Hampshire, where his nearly 400 weeks of lectures on a variety of topics related to the arts have garnered rave reviews from his participants, such as, "He is the Beethoven of lecturers"; "Magnificent! Electric! Inspiring!"; "The best teacher I've ever experienced." In 2005 he was honored by Elderhostel International as one of its most highly praised instructors.

Mr. Athnos received his degrees from Northwestern College in Minneapolis, Minnesota, and the University of Michigan, where he was elected to the National Music Honors Society. He also studied Norwegian folk music and its influence on Edvard Grieg at the University of Oslo. He has had 20 articles and poetry published in *Pro Musica* (the Music Journal of the former Yugoslavia), the *Mennonite Journal*, the *North Parker*, the *Covenant Companion*, and *Christianity and the Arts*. Mr. Athnos was a recipient of the *1990 Sears Foundation Award for Teaching Excellence and Campus Leadership*, and the *1992 Honorary Alumnus Award*, conferred by the Alumni Association of North Park University.

He has traveled throughout North America, Europe and Japan as conductor, guest clinician, and lecturer in music and theology, the latter emphasizing the theological significance of the Art of the Roman Catacombs. Two books were self-published through Outskirts Press in 2011: *"The Easter Jesus and the Good Friday Church: Reclaiming the Centrality of the Resurrection,"* awarded First Place in the 2014 *Christian Authors Awards* Theology category, and *"The Art of the Roman Catacombs: Themes of Deliverance in the Age of Persecution,"* awarded First Place in the History/Science category of the 2011 *Reader Views Literary Awards*. Both were acclaimed by *World Magazine* as the top two self-published books of 2011. In 2016 he published his autobiography, *"Eat in Harmony: A Feast of Life, the Arts, and Faith."* His fourth and fifth books are scheduled for publication in 2023: *"Handel's 'Messiah': A New View of its Musical & Spiritual Architecture—Study Guide for Listeners and Performers,"* and *"Silent Voices: Meditations for Holy Week, From the Palm Sunday Procession to the Easter Upper Room."*

Mr. Athnos retired from university teaching in 1998, and has kept a busy schedule of lectures and seminars for arts organizations, Elderhostel/Road Scholar, museums, conference centers, retirement communities, and churches.

Made in the USA
Monee, IL
16 June 2024

60000476R00066